Understanding Hope

Understanding Hope

A Brief Philosophical Exploration, Drawing on
Theology, Psychology, and Personal Loss

Philip D. Smith

CASCADE *Books* • Eugene, Oregon

UNDERSTANDING HOPE
A Brief Philosophical Exploration, Drawing on Theology, Psychology,
and Personal Loss

Cascade Books
An Imprint of Wipf and Stock Publishers
199 W. 8th Ave., Suite 3
Eugene, OR 97401

www.wipfandstock.com

PAPERBACK ISBN: 978-1-6667-1432-6
HARDCOVER ISBN: 978-1-6667-1433-3
EBOOK ISBN: 978-1-6667-1434-0

Cataloguing-in-Publication data:

Names: Smith, Philip D., author.

Title: Understanding hope : a brief philosophical exploration, drawing on theology, psychology, and personal loss / by Philip D. Smith.

Description: Eugene, OR : Cascade Books, 2022 | Includes bibliographical refer-
ences.

Identifiers: ISBN 978-1-6667-1432-6 (paperback) | ISBN 978-1-6667-1433-3 (hard-
cover) | ISBN 978-1-6667-1434-0 (ebook)

Subjects: LCSH: Hope.

Classification: BV4638 .S58 2022 (print) | BV4638 .S58 (ebook)

03/25/22

All quotations of the Bible are taken from the *New International Version*.
Zondervan, 2011.

This book is dedicated to my wife, Sarah Link. Before we met in 2018, we each experienced the death of a beloved spouse. Together we are exploring what it means to live in hope.

Contents

Preface

I 've been writing this book for seven years. That's not unusual for my philosophical work; I spent eight years on *The Virtue of Civility in the Practice of Politics* and eight more on *Why Faith Is a Virtue*. As a philosophy professor, my first priority is teaching. Writing conference papers and editing them into book chapters is important work mostly because it makes me a better teacher.

Almost all my philosophy papers address some aspect of what is called "virtue theory."

Since my graduate school days, I have thought that Christians ought to welcome the late-twentieth-century revival of virtue theory. Therefore, I have written about love, civility, faith, and now hope. I have never hesitated to draw on theology for cues for my philosophical work.

If we want to think well about the virtues, philosophers must pay attention to psychology. We must not simply accept what they say, but a critical reading of psychological theory can lead to insight. Or at least, it may keep us from making silly mistakes. For much of my teaching career, I had the advantage of a psychologist spouse who could criticize my ideas.

In 2016, two years into my hope project, Karen died. Two years after that, I married Sarah. Philosophy has to be rooted in the life we actually live. (According to one story, Kierkegaard remarked about Hegel: "Someone should remind the philosopher he just ate breakfast." Even if the story isn't true, it gives insight into Kierkegaard and Hegel.) What I offer in this book about hope draws on personal experience as much as the authors I cite.

Acknowledgments

I began work on this book in 2014, using a faculty sabbatical from George Fox University. I am grateful not only for sabbatical support, but also for travel and conference funds that allowed me to read papers at the Northwest Conference on Philosophy and the Pacific-Mountain Conference of the Society of Christian Philosophers, papers which became parts of chapters 4 and 5.

At the 2016 SCP conference, I benefited from conversation with Mark Bernier, who helped me think about Kierkegaard's view of hope. Thanks also to Ross McCullough and other colleagues at GFU, who have given feedback on portions of the text. And I thank my students who took a philosophy/literature course called "Life Well Lived" in the years 2017–21; their response to the "Last Walk" essays convinced me to include those essays in the book.

1

What Is Hope?

I n 2008, Barack Obama's campaign for president energized a new generation of voters with the slogan "hope and change." Given the partisan nature of politics in America, his opponents were happy to mock Obama's slogan in 2010 and again in 2014. In various ways they asked voters, "Is this what you hoped for? Is this the change you wanted?"

Obama's campaign wasn't the first time hope played an explicit role in American politics. An older generation of voters can remember 1992, when Bill Clinton's campaign presented him as "the man from Hope," playing on Clinton's hometown in Arkansas.

Politicians don't have to use the word "hope" to incorporate this theme. In 1984, Ronald Reagan's campaign famously trumpeted, "It's morning in America," and asked voters why they would want to go back to the bad, dark times before Reagan's first election. The message was not just that economic indicators had improved under Reagan; the "morning in America" slogan emphasized a change in collective feeling, from the pessimism of the Carter years to the ebullient optimism of Reagan.

Going back further, historians and economists debate whether Franklin Roosevelt's programs to lift the country out of the Great Depression really worked. But they almost all agree that Roosevelt's confidence and sunny disposition, which he masterfully communicated in radio talks, helped Americans believe in a better future.

Some political commentators claim that this appeal to hope resonates deeply and uniquely with the American spirit. "The only thing we have to fear is fear itself," Roosevelt said. Americans loved that, perhaps more than other peoples. I have no evidence that the United States is any different from other countries in this regard; it seems almost axiomatic that candidates for office will claim that things will get better if they are elected and their policies enacted. In America at least, and maybe universally, hopefulness would seem to be an asset to politicians.

I point to these examples not to begin a study of politics, but to invite the reader to consider this concept of hope. Outside of politics, many people are familiar with hope as an important word in religion, psychology, and philosophy. Consider just a few particulars.

Religion. The New Testament often mentions hope along with other traits that should mark Christian character. In 1 Corinthians 13:13, Paul contrasts three qualities that "remain"—faith, hope, and love—with "spiritual gifts," such as speaking in tongues or prophecy. Later theologians classified faith, hope, and love as "virtues." Paul seems to teach that these virtues are more important than spiritual gifts.[1]

Paul says further, "The greatest of these is love." Christian thinkers ever since have worked to understand faith, hope, and love and how they relate to each other. Thomas Aquinas wrote that faith, hope, and love were theological virtues, distinguished from the natural virtues, such as courage and temperance, because faith, hope, and love had God as their object and were infused in the believer by God. In our time, theologians like N. T. Wright, Jürgen Moltmann, and David Elliot argue that hope should be seen as a central feature in Christian theology and ethics.

Psychology. In recent decades the broad movement called positive psychology has included an emphasis on hope. For example, C. R. Snyder and his colleagues introduced "hope theory," a particular and definite way to say what hope is, and "hope therapy," practical interventions based on the theory. They have conducted an enormous amount of empirical research showing that hopefulness correlates well with positive life outcomes. Therapeutic interventions that increase hopefulness, as measured by simple "hope scales," fairly reliably improve life for patients. Another team of psychologists, Anthony Scioli and Henry Biller, argue for a broader understanding of hope than Snyder's cognitive approach. They agree with Snyder that hope is a crucial component of good living, going so far as to say hope is "our most important" virtue.

Philosophy. Immanuel Kant famously included hope among the three foundational questions of philosophy: What can I know? What ought I to

---

1. We might do well to meditate on the contrast between virtues (traits of character) and gifts (abilities or powers to perform). The churches need the latter, but even more they need people of good character.

do? For what may I hope? The twentieth-century Christian existentialist Gabriel Marcel saw hope as central to his response to the crisis of modern life. Philosophers in the Thomist tradition, such as Josef Pieper and David Elliot, have extended Aquinas's analysis of hope. More recently, in 2006, Jonathan Lear invited readers to consider "radical hope," which he found exemplified in the life of Chief Plenty Coups, the last great chief of the Crow nation. More recently still, in 2014, Adrienne Martin explored hope as a paradigm virtue in *How We Hope: A Moral Psychology.*

In this book I will borrow ideas from most of these sources and many others. As an analytic philosopher, I seek to write clearly first of all; philosophical confusions often arise from sloppy use of language, language "gone on holiday" in Ludwig Wittgenstein's words. But I also hold the old-fashioned idea that philosophy, especially moral philosophy, ought to be practical; it ought to make a difference. I intend that my work in moral philosophy, including this book on hope, will aid readers in their quest to live good lives. I intend that this book be both *clear* and *helpful.*

It is already apparent that hope is an important concept. But questions surround it. What is hope, exactly? Are all these authors—theologians, psychologists, philosophers—talking about the same thing? Almost everyone seems to think hope is a good thing. Why is that? (We will see in chapter 3 that some philosophers have been pretty skeptical about hope.) Are there different kinds of hope? If so, are some hopes more important than others? Can a person do something to make herself hopeful, or does hope simply happen to her? Is it possible that a person could have a "task" of hope, a phrase suggested by Søren Kierkegaard? What is the relationship between hope and fear? Are there connections between hope and other virtues, in particular faith and love?

And so on. The goal of this book is to answer at least some of these questions. Though I do not believe that hope is the "most important" virtue, a philosophical exploration of hope can be of real practical help. By answering some questions about hope, we can live better lives.

Defining Hope: The Central Idea

In one sense, everyone is familiar with hope. Consider Thomas Aquinas's example of a dog. If the dog sees a rabbit too far away, it won't chase the rabbit, because it has no hope of catching it. But if the quarry is closer, the dog chases it, hoping to catch it. When the dog catches the rabbit, he no longer hopes, because he has what he wanted.[2]

Aquinas's dog illustrates essential aspects of hope. First, the dog *wants* the rabbit. Secondly, the dog thinks or *judges* that it might catch the rabbit. Thus, Aquinas taught, hope combines two different capacities, *appetite* and *intellect*. I will explore both aspects of hope a few paragraphs hence.

Since Socrates, philosophers have taught that people only desire things they judge to be good. Hope, therefore, is directed toward the *good* (or what a person thinks is good). Second, the dog's desire for the rabbit is for something he *does not* have. Sometimes we desire things we already have, as when I desire to be with my family while eating Thanksgiving dinner with them. Hope's desire, unlike desires for things I have already, is directed toward the *future*.

Someone might contest this last thought. An objector could claim that we sometimes hope for things that have already happened. For example, consider a family whose loved one was a passenger on an airplane that has gone missing. They have received no news about whether the plane crashed or about possible survivors. Don't we say that they *hope* that the plane landed safely, or that their loved one survived the crash, if there were a crash? Isn't this a hope for something in the past rather than the future? No. It will be less confusing to say the family hopes *to learn* there were no crash or that their loved one has survived, so that their hope is directed toward the future. It is clearer to say we might *wish* that the past had been different than it was, but we don't hope for a different past. I will say more about the difference between wishing and hoping in chapter 5.

The dog judges that it *may* catch the rabbit. Hope's desire and judgment is directed toward *possible* things. We don't hope for things that are impossible (the rabbit that is too far away) or things that are already achieved (the rabbit already caught). Hope, then, combines appetite and judgment directed toward *possible future goods*. Is that enough?

Aquinas would say that to this point we have only described a natural passion, something we share with animals, which must be distinguished from the true virtue of hope. That poses another set of questions: How does a passion differ from a virtue? What is a virtue, after all? Why does Aquinas call hope a "theological" virtue? I will return to these questions in a bit.

For the moment, the crucial point concerns *appetite* and *intellect*. Aquinas thought these features of natural hope carried over to the virtue

---

2. Aquinas, *Summa Theologiae* I–II.40.3, in Andre, "Summa Theologica."

of hope; the theological virtue of hope, though focused on something very different than natural hopes, also combines appetite (our desire for friendship with God) and intellect (the belief that friendship with God might be achieved).

Let's think about the judgment aspect of hope first. We need not suppose that Aquinas's dog "reasoned" about the likelihood of catching the rabbit. The dog's judgment, "close enough!"—occurs automatically, perhaps instinctually. In many cases this is true of human hopes as well. A driver accelerates toward an intersection, hoping to get through before the light turns; she's thinking about arriving on time for an appointment, not explicitly judging the likelihood of catching the light. For both the dog and the driver, hope's judgment is implicit. In other cases, the intellectual component of hope is explicit and conscious, as when a patient listens to a surgeon explaining the odds of success for a certain procedure before deciding whether to have surgery.

Philosophers, naturally, are interested in the judgment aspect of hope. Some of them—Simon Critchley, for example—warn against hope. Too often, these cautionary philosophers say, we judge badly. We overestimate our chances of achieving some good end and act foolishly, thus subjecting ourselves to evils that could have been easily avoided. On this account, hope is a dangerous thing, because it is often irrational. I will discuss the rationality of hope in chapter 3.

Now let's think about the desire component of hope. As Aquinas noted, hopes differ according to the thing for which we hope. Borrowing a term from environmentalist philosopher John Nolt, I will call the hoped-for future good an "object-state."[3] The object-state for Aquinas's dog is catching the rabbit; the object-state for the driver trying to beat the stoplight is to arrive at her destination on time. For Nolt and some other environmental ethicists, their most desired object-state is impossible to achieve, because what they truly desire is that human activity had not polluted the environment in the last 200 years. This creates anxiety for Nolt and his fellow writers, since they have no hope for their greatest desire. (They might *wish* that human beings had not polluted the atmosphere with greenhouse gases over the last two centuries, but they cannot *hope* it had not happened.) Nevertheless, they see that hope is a good thing—or, perhaps more accurately, they see that hope *could* be a good thing, if we hope for the right things in

---

3. Nolt, "Hope, Self-Transcendence, and Environmental Ethics," 47.

the right way. I will discuss the environmentalist philosophers' ambivalence further in chapter 3.

This minimal idea of hope—that hope consists in desire for some future possible good—will need to be refined. Consider how greatly object-states can vary.

Number: an object-state may concern only one person, as when a student hopes for a good mark on a test; a group of people, as when a work team hopes their project will succeed; or even the whole world, as we hope the world can transition to environmentally safe sources of energy. *Moral status*: object-states may be pernicious, as when a drug kingpin hopes to escape prison, kill his rivals, and resume control of his cartel; morally ambiguous, such as my hope that the Mariners defeat your team in the World Series; or morally praiseworthy, as when a firefighter hopes to prevent loss of life. *Practical importance*: sometimes we hope for trivial things, as when a teenager hopes for a new high score on a computer game; other hopes seem critically important if we want to live good lives, e.g., avoiding nuclear war.

Aquinas would add another contrast or aspect in which hopes differ, the distinction between *temporal* and *eternal* hopes. Hopes for this world, even friendship with God, are "imperfect." Our greatest and highest hope aims at perfected friendship with God in heaven. Properly speaking, on Aquinas's terms, the true virtue of hope focuses on God, so hopes for earthly goods (money, prestige, a quiet and peaceful life, meaningful labor, etc.) are examples of hope as a passion.

Since human beings are morally and epistemically flawed, we sometimes desire things that are not actually good or good for us, so it is possible to hope for things that are objectively evil. In 1939, Hitler did not want a replay of the Czechoslovakia episode; he hoped that his invasion of Poland would start a war with France and Britain. Hitler foolishly and evilly regarded war in the fall of 1939 as a good thing.

Since human beings are often unreflective and sometimes irrational, some of our object-states contradict some of our other object-states, so it is possible for a person to hope for two object-states such that the occurrence of one precludes the other. Both hoped-for object-states may be genuinely good things. There is not enough room in a single human life to collect all the good things a person may hope for. I will discuss moral limitations on hopes and the idea of a "central" hope later in the book.

What I have said so far justifies an observation: hope is complicated. Nevertheless, I offer a preliminary "core definition" of hope: *hope is a desire for a future object-state thought to be good and judged (implicitly or explicitly) to be possible (neither certain nor impossible).*

The Ubiquity of Hope

Given the core definition, almost all human deliberate actions are "hopeful," because we act to gain some end. I prepare a meal because I want to eat and/or I want to provide food for others. I exercise because I want better health and the endorphin "high" I've learned to expect from jogging. I sign an auto loan because I want to drive a new car. I contract with a publisher because I want readers to read my book. Such deliberate actions of agents contrast with instinctual reactions (blinking in bright light) or autonomic bodily functions (the beating of the heart, the digestion of food). When we act deliberately, unless we are certain to achieve our desired object-state, we act in hope.

Sometimes people act to avoid some object-state, out of fear or disgust. I decide not to drive tonight because it is snowing heavily. While walking through the countryside I keep distance from the carcass of a dead animal. These are deliberate actions, and they aim at avoiding something we judge as bad. Such actions, motivated by fear or disgust, are the flip side of hope. Occasionally in this book, it will be helpful to describe such actions as hopeful, in the sense that we hope to *avoid or escape* future object-states judged to be bad. Sometimes we don't know exactly what we want, but we know clearly what we don't want.

The core definition and the ubiquity of hope help explain why almost everyone thinks it is a good thing. Without hope, we rarely act. *Hopelessness* comes in degrees, and the more extreme forms have long been recognized as spiritual or psychological disorders, i.e., despair and depression. When a person loses all hope he no longer expects good outcomes from his actions. Why act when nothing good will come of it? Without hope of some form in some degree, a person may cease to be an agent at all.

What Is a Virtue?

In spite of some philosophers' demurrals (see chapter 3), most people readily think of hope as a good thing. It saves us from despair, and it sustains us in the pursuit of difficult goals. In Christianity, hope is traditionally listed among the "virtues." Before going further, then, we need to clarify that concept. What is a virtue?

In an earlier book, *Why Faith Is a Virtue*, I spent fifteen pages explaining Alasdair MacIntyre's definition of virtues, given in his influential book, *After Virtue*, and I included a discussion of Robert Adams's comments on the intrinsic value of virtues in his book, *A Theory of Virtue*. Rather than repeat that exposition, I give here a modified summary of those pages:

1. Moral virtues are characteristics of *human beings*. Animals, extraterrestrials, or angels may have virtues appropriate to their kinds, but moral philosophy focuses on people.

2. Virtues are *acquired*, as opposed to natural gifts like visual acuity or physical beauty; acquisition of virtues usually takes time and effort.

3. Virtues are enduring *tendencies*, neither isolated incidents nor ironclad laws of behavior. We say a person is honest if she dependably tells the truth, not just once in a while. But we may describe her as honest even if she fails to be truthful in rare situations.

4. Particular virtues will have *differing* psychological structures, involving emotions, desires, beliefs, and intentions in varying ways. (I will say more about the psychology of hope in chapter 4.)

5. Virtues are *intrinsically* valuable. (Robert Adams contends for this point, and I think he is right. Nevertheless, the intrinsic value of virtues did not factor in my argument in *Why Faith Is a Virtue*. I will make some comments on the intrinsic value of hope in chapter 7.)

6. Virtues are *instrumentally* valuable. They help us achieve good outcomes in at least three different ways: *a*) virtues tend to help us achieve the internal goods of practices; *b*) virtues tend to help individuals as they seek for unity in their lives, a unity that gives meaning to the practices they engage in; and *c*) virtues tend to sustain practices and traditions over time, giving background and context to individuals' pursuit of good lives.[4]

Not every philosopher in the virtue tradition would agree with each of these points. For instance, Homer and other ancient Greek authors counted physical strength and beauty among the *arête*; such natural qualities are not acquired but are gifts of nature or God. Over time, natural gifts

---

4. Smith, *Why Faith Is a Virtue*, 1–17.

dropped out of the lists of recognized virtues. Thomas Aquinas thought that faith, hope, and love (the theological virtues) were "infused" in believers by God's grace. If that is right, we needn't think of "acquiring" virtues exclusively as something we do; we may acquire something by receiving it from another (God).[5] In general, however, points 1–4 are uncontroversial among philosophers.

Point 5 bothers some naturalistically minded thinkers; it sounds too much like Plato's notion of transcendent "forms." Now, I do think virtues are intrinsically valuable, and I agree with Robert Adams's theistic theory of ultimate value. But readers will be able to benefit from studying hope even if they believe hope has only instrumental value.

Point 6 contains MacIntyre's attempt to give an instrumental theory of virtue, a theory he claims captures the historical core of the virtue tradition. On MacIntyre's account, a character trait is a virtue if its possession tends to help people get good results. In *Why Faith Is a Virtue*, I argued that faith, rightly understood, is a virtue precisely in those terms. I argued that faith helps people gain the *internal goods* of *practices* (important terms for MacIntyre), namely scientific research, social reform, and parenting.

MacIntyre claims that his definition of virtues expresses the heart of the virtue tradition, a golden thread that runs through the thought of ancient writers like Aristotle, medieval thinkers like Aquinas, and modern writers like Jane Austen. I think he's right. MacIntyre's instrumental definition of virtues, highlighted in point 6 above, will guide the discussion in this book.

Hope as Passion and Virtue

A central idea in *After Virtue* is MacIntyre's claim, which seems manifestly true, that the virtue tradition developed over time. Some traits that were regarded as human excellences (*arête*) in the Homeric literature, such as physical strength, ceased to be regarded as virtues later on. Later stages in the virtue tradition introduced new virtues. Crucially, the New Testament identifies faith, hope, and love as virtues.

Before the New Testament period, Aristotle did write about hope, but not as a virtue. On Aristotle's account, hope is a characteristic of young

---

5. Aquinas modifies Aristotle's account on this point. Aristotle said that we gain the virtues through practicing them, i.e., habituation. But Aquinas thought the theological virtues come to us from God, though we must practice them as well.

men who look forward to accomplishing great things. Old men no longer hope; instead, their lives are marked by *memory* of deeds attempted and perhaps accomplished. Virtues are traits that help us live better lives, presumably at every stage of life. On his view, then, since hope helps only young persons, hope is not a virtue.

This created a problem for Thomas Aquinas, who built much of his work on Aristotle. The great philosopher (often Aquinas does not name Aristotle, merely saying "the philosopher") did not list as virtues those traits the New Testament identifies as the most important. How could Aristotle fail to notice the most important virtues? Aquinas solved this problem by classifying faith, hope, and love as "theological virtues." The theological virtues are actually the highest and most important, because they help us gain the highest good, eternal friendship and enjoyment of God. Aristotle, as a pagan philosopher, was ignorant of Christ. So, Aquinas thought, Aristotle's insights into ethics were limited to natural life and the goods of this world, whereas faith, hope, and love direct us to our supernatural life and the goods of the world to come. Aristotle's remarks about hope apply only to the natural passion of hope, not the theological virtue.

Aquinas's solution suggests an interesting question. If temporal goods were the only goods, then Aristotle's remark about young men hoping and old men remembering seems plausible. We may ask, then, *is* hope a virtue for older persons? Can naturalistic philosophers, who hold that temporal, this-worldly goods *are* the only goods, defend hope as a virtue for persons nearing the end of life? Perhaps. I will explore Jonathan Lear's idea of "radical hope" in chapter 5. Later, in chapter 7, I will accuse naturalistic philosophy of excluding most transcendent hopes.

Meanwhile, on the distinction between passion and virtue, Charles Pinches approvingly quotes Josef Pieper, who wrote: "It would never occur to a philosopher, unless he were a Christian theologian, to describe hope as a virtue. For hope is either a theological virtue or not a virtue at all."[6]

Now, in one sense, Pieper's claim is simply false. Jonathan Lear and Adrienne Martin, whose contributions I will discuss in later chapters, are contemporary philosophers who have written insightfully about hope. They are not Christian theologians. Why would Pieper make such an obvious mistake? Why would Pinches agree with him?

Because of the passion/virtue distinction, that's why. Pinches and Pieper are cleaving to Aquinas's doctrine. On this account, real hope

6. Pinches, "On Hope," 349.

focuses on God and is engendered in us ("infused") by God, and the thing that Jonathan Lear and Adrienne Martin write about is properly the passion of hope, not the virtue of hope.

Can we learn something from this dispute about words? Yes. There are different kinds of hope, distinguished by their differing object-states. By comparing and contrasting different kinds of hope we may better see how hope may function in our lives. In spite of endorsing Pieper, Charles Pinches agrees on this point. Pinches says that Aquinas's comments on the natural passion of hope can teach us about the theological virtue of hope.[7]

On Aquinas's view, the passion of hope is directed toward something we desire in this world, and there is no guarantee that human beings will desire the right things. Sometimes we hope for trivial things: I confess that I hope much for a Mariners pennant; someone else might hope to find a new knick-knack at the flea market. Such hopes seem innocent enough, though we recoil from scenes of soccer fans rioting after matches. We should guard against hoping too much for small things. More importantly, human beings sometimes desire objectively evil things. A fraudster may hope to escape detection or conviction. A slave owner may hope to capture his runaway slave. Don Juan may hope to seduce his neighbor. So natural hope, hope as a passion, might not always be a good thing. Aquinas, following Aristotle, thought that a virtue ought to "perfect" us, that is, help make us what we truly ought to be. Since the natural passion of hope can easily go wrong, we ought not to list it among the virtues.

The theological virtue of hope cannot go wrong in these ways, thought Aquinas. The virtue of hope focuses on God, our true end. Hope sustains pilgrims; we journey through opposition and difficulties toward a very great good. We cannot truly hope—that is, hope as a virtue—for something that is opposed to that goal.

Aquinas described a movement among the theological virtues. By *faith* a person comes to believe that God exists and rewards those who seek God; the soul becomes aware of the highest good. In *hope* a person desires that great good and moves toward it; since our journey toward God lasts throughout this life, hope is a virtue for all stages of life. In contrast to Aristotle's observation, Christian hope is appropriate for every part of this life. When it comes to the theological virtue of hope, we are all young. *Love* is the culmination of faith and hope; in love we are joined to God in friendship now and forever.

7. Pinches, "On Hope," 352.

The overarching goal of the moral life according to Aristotle is *eudaimonia*, or "happiness." Aquinas approved of Aristotle's theory as far as it went. But Aristotle's notion of happiness aims only at goods in this world. What Aristotle's theory leaves out, Aquinas said, is that we have a supernatural end. Our true end is not earthly happiness (though that is a great good), but heavenly beatitude. The theological virtues—faith, hope, and love—prepare us for blessedness.[8]

Aquinas recognized a similarity in structure between the natural passion of hope and the theological virtue of hope. Natural hope desires some earthly good and helps a person overcome obstacles that might keep her from attaining that good. But the true virtue of hope focuses on our highest good, eternal fellowship with God.

In this book I will speak of hope as a virtue in a wider sense than Aquinas. If it is true that eternal fellowship with God is our highest good (and I agree that it is), then hope that focuses on that good is a very important hope indeed. With Aquinas we can call it theological hope. But hopes for earthly goods are still hopes, and I will argue that the Christian gospel urges us to pursue many earthly goods. I think it is proper to classify hope for some earthly object-states as a virtue.

Which earthly hopes are true virtues?

Clearly, people can hope for evil things. If hope is to be a virtue, our earlier analysis of hope needs a codicil: *at a minimum, hope must focus on morally permissible objects.* Don Juan's hope to bed his neighbor is a vice, not a virtue. Further, *truly praiseworthy hope ought to focus on genuinely good things.* My hopes for a Mariners pennant are innocent, but they don't seem to link up with objective good in the way praiseworthy hope should.

New Testament scholars agree that Jesus' preaching centered on the kingdom of God: "The kingdom of God is at hand! Repent, and believe the good news!" (Mark 1:15). Bible scholars tell us that "the kingdom" is not just a code phrase for the afterlife. In context, this New Testament phrase carries much freight: "the kingdom of God is . . . righteousness, peace, and joy in the Holy Spirit" (Rom 14:17). When we pray for God's kingdom to come, we pray for God's will to be done. We enter the kingdom now, we live as its citizens here, and we also eagerly wait for its fulfillment in heaven. *Hope is a virtue when we hope for the kingdom of God.* Eternal friendship with God in heaven, yes; but we also hope for God's will to be done on earth.

---

8. Drefeinski, "Very Short Primer."

I will discuss "kingdom hope" further in chapter 8, but one implication of "kingdom hope" should be mentioned now.

If the kingdom of God includes God's will being done on earth, then people of non-Christian faith and people of no faith at all may exhibit genuine hope. They would not use Christian terms such as "kingdom of God" to describe their hopes, and atheists would not associate their hopes with God in any way. But to the extent that they hope for peace, justice, or the renewal of the earth, their hopes link up with the virtue of hope in its highest sense.

Summary

Hope (whether a passion or virtue) aims at an object-state judged to be good and possible. The *virtue of hope* aims for an object-state that is genuinely good and possible. The object-states aimed at by the virtue of hope must not conflict with the highest and best hope. The *theological virtue of hope* aims at the highest possible good, eternal friendship with and enjoyment of God. If God exists, this is the highest and best hope; if God does not exist, the object-states aimed at by virtuous hopes might fall into conceptual confusion, unless some other highest and best hope could be identified.

2

Who Needs Hope?

W ith some exceptions (see chapter 3), most people assume hope is a good thing. Medical doctors, politicians, psychologists, and theologians all agree that hope helps us achieve better lives. To begin with, hope *feels* good; almost everyone would prefer the "up" of hopefulness to the "down" of despair or depression. More importantly, since hope focuses on a future good, it can help us stay on course toward that good even when we are experiencing difficulties. This second feature of hope, its power to sustain a person in pursuit of an arduous good, deserves most of our attention. The question "Who needs hope?" is answered "Anyone who desires a good difficult to attain." A little reflection will show that includes all of us.

The *Eudaimonia* Gap

David Elliot, in *Hope and Christian Ethics*, uses the label "*eudaimonia* gap" to describe our need for hope.[1] The gap is the difference between the good lives rational persons desire and the lives they actually live. As rational persons, they see that the good lives they desire are possible, yet they also see they don't yet have them. They are hindered from the good lives they want by a variety of factors.

In Aristotle and other ancient Greek authors, *eudaimonia* names the proper goal of human living. The usual English translation, "happiness," understates the rich content of *eudaimonia*. For Aristotle, *eudaimonia* meant feeling well, but also doing well in a way that generates feeling well. In recent decades philosophers writing in English have started using "flourishing" to better represent Aristotle's intent. *Eudaimonia* is a state of

1. Elliot, *Hope and Christian Ethics*, 15.

well-being resulting from successful participation in activities appropriate to creatures like us.

We can start by imagining the kind of life Aristotle had in mind. A citizen of Athens or some other Greek city-state would be a farmer, an architect, a shipbuilder, a tradesman, a potter, a writer, a teacher, a priest, or some other occupation. In addition to such economic roles, the citizen might participate in religious ceremonies, attend the theater (dramas or comedies), watch athletic events such as the Olympic games, listen to public lectures or debates, and participate in government by voting, serving on juries, engaging in military service, holding public office, etc. Fundamental to a citizen's life, more basic in one sense than his economic or public roles, would be his family connections as a son, descendent of a particular *deme*, husband of his wife, father to his children, and master to any servants in the household. Every aspect of a citizen's life—family, economic, and especially public—afforded opportunities for the citizen to establish and enjoy friendship, which Aristotle prized as an especially great good. Aristotle's view of a good life for a human being, a life of *eudaimonia*, was a rich, complex whole.

Notice that the roles of the "citizen" in the last paragraph are male roles: husband, father, juror, priest, etc. Like almost everyone else in ancient Greece, Aristotle took traditional gender roles for granted.[2] As a philosopher, he reasoned there must be an underlying natural cause for the difference between men and women, and he offered a theory: in the womb male fetuses were hotter while females were cooler. Because of their "hotter" blood, men were naturally disposed to strenuous, intellectual, and public activities. Women were naturally fit for childbearing and ordering private homes.

I draw attention to Aristotle's view of the sexes not as an historical illustration of sexism (though it is that), but as an illustration of luck (*tuchê*). Can a woman live a good life? Can she achieve *eudaimonia*? Aristotle's answer: only to a degree. On his view, women are by nature less rational than men, less able to participate in the fine activities that make up a truly happy life. Now, a person cannot choose her sex. On Aristotle's view, if a person is born a woman, she is simply unlucky.

For Aristotle, the distinction between male and female is only one example of luck. Consider politics. One of the great advantages of a Greek

---

2. In the *Republic*, Plato allowed that women might be philosophers and "guardians," the most important role in the state. But the ideal state of *Republic* contrasts sharply with actual roles of women in the Greek city-states.

city-state, such as Athens, was that citizens could actively participate in government with a reasonable expectation that their voice would be heard.[3] In contrast, a man born in a barbarian tribe could not enjoy the settled life of a city, while a man born under despotism (e.g., the Persian Empire) had no say in public affairs. Worldwide, it turns out that only a tiny percentage of men in Aristotle's day were lucky enough to have opportunity for rewarding participation in politics, and this diminished their chances of *eudaimonia*.

Consider wealth. Among the virtues, Aristotle lists *megalopsychia*, the characteristic of the "great man." The great man attempts great deeds; sometimes he gives great gifts. (Think of a modern billionaire philanthropist.) The great man's wealth frees him to support the theater, commission sculptures, endow political causes, and so on. Perhaps he will use his leisure to devote himself to the highest of human aspirations: contemplative philosophy, the pursuit of wisdom (*sophia*). Aristotle sees *megalopsychia* as a true moral virtue. Merely having wealth is not enough; the rich man will have to train himself in *megalopsychia* just as a soldier will have to train himself in courage. However, most men—and this is the point—can only admire *megalopsychia* from a distance, since they do not have great wealth. They are unlucky.

We begin to see that, on Aristotle's account, the good life (*eudaimonia*) is very often constrained by factors outside a person's control. What we might call the lottery of birth determines one's sex and strongly influences one's chances at political influence or wealth. Further, even if a person is born as a wealthy male Athenian, luck might undermine *eudaimonia* through disease, disability, war, natural disasters, political upheaval, or betrayal by business or political allies. Luck, *tuchê*, is "what just happens." The uncontrolled events of life often threaten the good lives we want to live.

At the university where I teach, I introduce the topic of *tuchê* by handing out 3x5 cards and asking students to list five things they would like to do or experience in their lives. The items they list are predictable: making money, gaining advanced degrees, pursuing a good career, traveling, experiencing romance and marriage, having children, participating meaningfully in government or social movements, accomplishing artistic goals, and so on. On the reverse side of the cards, I ask the students to write two impediments that might prevent them from achieving their goals. Typical responses include

3. Ironically, Aristotle lived as a foreigner in Athens. He could observe and theorize about Athenian democracy, but he could not vote or hold office.

lack of money, failure at a job, inability to gain entrance to grad school, injury from an accident, debilitating disease, and early death. With a little prompting, they also recognize global climate change, political upheavals, and war as possible large-scale impediments to their plans.

In her study of ancient Greek philosophy and drama, *The Fragility of Goodness*, Martha Nussbaum argues that *tuchê* is not confined to external forces like poverty, disease, or war. *Tuchê* also shows up in desperate moral choices.[4] Classic Greek tragedies give us protagonists—Oedipus, Agamemnon, Antigone, and others—who seem doomed to make impossible choices, damned if they choose one way and damned if they choose the other. *Oedipus the King*: As king of Thebes, Oedipus must find and punish the man who killed his father, not knowing that he himself was the killer. Aeschylus's *Agamemnon*: As commander of the Greek fleet gathered to set sail against Troy, Agamemnon must first appease a goddess who requires that he sacrifice his daughter, Iphigenia. If the fleet does not sail, Agamemnon disobeys the gods and courts mutiny among the men, but if he sacrifices Iphigenia, he commits plain murder of an innocent girl. *Antigone*: Antigone's brothers, Polynices and Eteocles, have been killed in battle outside the city walls. The king declares that Eteocles, who died defending the city, should have an honorable burial, but Polynices, who led the invading army and was a traitor to Thebes, must lie unburied as carrion for birds. Antigone must either disobey King Creon or violate her family duty to Polynices.

If ancient tragedies don't grip the modern soul, consider a more contemporary example, *Sophie's Choice* (novel by William Styron, prize-winning 1982 movie). Amidst the horror of a Nazi death camp, a guard invents a new level of sadism: he tells a young mother to choose which of her children will be sent to the gas chamber and which allowed to live. Though she survived the war, Sophie is racked by guilt; though compelled to choose, *she did choose*. She immigrates to America but eventually she commits suicide with her schizophrenic lover.

The lottery of birth, uncontrollable circumstances like disease or accidents, and tragic situations that compel persons to decide between one evil and another: David Elliot calls this the "negative side" of the *eudaimonia* gap. Very often in life "what just happens" frustrates our desires for good lives. As rational beings we can imagine ourselves living better lives, in a readily understandable sense we see those good lives as *possible*, and yet factors outside our control keep us from living those lives. People may

4. Nussbaum, *Fragility of Goodness*, 7, 30–41.

not think this way—that is, in terms of a "gap" between their desires and their actual circumstances—but we readily understand the notion of the "pursuit of happiness." Many people are very aware of circumstances that stand between them and happiness.

In addition to the negative *eudaimonia* gap, Elliot says there is a "positive side" to the gap.[5] This is the contrast between a pretty good life and an even better life. Imagine a person of good *tuchê*. She has good health, lives in a stable society, has benefited from education, participates in challenging and interesting work, enjoys rewarding relationships, and has not suffered the "slings and arrows of outrageous fortune." This person has not faced desperate choices and can look back on her life without much guilt. To a very large extent, she has escaped the effects of war, disease, or disability. She has been, and knows she has been, lucky. Still, Elliot says, such a person knows that her world could be better. On a personal level, she may desire greater recognition in her field, new and bigger successes, more wealth, and similar goods for her children. But her desires are not limited to herself and her family. She cares about other people, so injustice and poverty move her to desire political and social changes. She desires that other people, including people living far away, have opportunities to learn and enjoy the beauty of the world. She wants a healthy environment worldwide rather than one poisoned by pollution or ruined by climate change. In sum: though she knows that in comparison to most people on earth she lives a "happy" life, she still desires "more" or "better."

The vast majority of people on earth experience the negative side of the *eudaimonia* gap, and those fortunate enough to escape the negative side still face the positive side of the gap. Elliot's summary claim is this: on reflection, we all experience the *eudaimonia* gap. *We all want something better than what we have.* How should we respond to this truth?

Closing the Gap by Trimming Desires

David Elliot's label, "*eudaimonia* gap," was invented recently. But the problem has been recognized for millennia, and at least two very different responses have been proposed. The first, which comes in a number of guises and under various names, says our problem lies in our desires. If we learn to desire the right things, this advice says, we will find we can have

5. Elliot, *Hope and Christian Ethics*, 43–45.

them. It is only when we desire the wrong things, things subject to luck, that we create the gap.

In *The Fragility of Goodness*, Martha Nussbaum considers Platonist and Stoic answers to the problem of *tuchê*. For Platonists, real knowledge is knowledge of the eternal forms (beauty, justice, goodness), and the good life consists in coming to "see" the forms. As Diotima taught Socrates (in Plato's *Symposium*), the wise person moves from the love of beauty of one body to the love of the beauty of all bodies, and then to the love of Beauty itself (the form of the beautiful). Once the wise person sees true Beauty, the physical world of bodies and pleasures—and the threats to bodies from disease or death—isn't very important.[6]

For the Stoic, the good life is a rational life, lived in accord with universal reason (*logos*). Pain, death, betrayal—none of that matters for the mind that is ruled by reason. For Platonist and Stoic alike, one can escape the power of *tuchê* through proper philosophy. We can train ourselves in a kind of good life that is impervious to luck.

Surprisingly, a similar response to the *eudaimonia* gap can be found in ancient Epicureanism. Since Epicurus taught that the good life was a life of pleasure, one would think that such a good life would be especially susceptible to bad luck. (Imagine the fictional gourmand, Nero Wolfe, sitting down to a much-anticipated feast and discovering the vegetables were slightly overcooked.) But Epicurus denied that his doctrine of pleasure led to a life of parties and excess. Real pleasure, he wrote, consisted in "repose" (*ataraxia*), the absence of pain in the body or trouble in the mind. Most trouble in the mind comes from desiring too much. Epicurus thought we can be genuinely happy if we learn to be content with having enough.

Though unmentioned by Nussbaum, the same general response to human unhappiness is found in Buddhism. The Four Noble Truths teach that human suffering arises from our desires, but our desires can be corrected, and the eightfold path details ways to correct them. It is no surprise that statues of the Buddha show him smiling; the person who has achieved enlightenment is no longer held captive by desire, and therefore he is happy.

Very often, Christian thought has tended in the same direction. In the words of a twentieth-century song, "This world is not my home; I'm just a-passing through." The idea is that we will never be content if we focus

---

6. Nussbaum locates this "Platonist" answer in *Symposium* and *Protagoras*. She argues that Plato himself, in *Phaedrus*, questioned the too-neat answer given by Socrates in *Protagoras* and Diotima in *Symposium*.

our desires on this world, but this does not matter because our true goal is heaven. We can defeat the *eudaimonia* gap by redirecting our desires from this world to the next. Marxists have often criticized Christianity for using this line of thinking as a tool to oppress the poor. Religion, Marx wrote, was the "opiate of the people," that kept them focused on next-worldly rewards while the rich enjoyed this world's goods.

Whether or not Marx's sociopolitical accusation against Christianity was accurate, it raises an important question: What should Christians hope for? Does Christianity teach us to eliminate the *eudaimonia* gap by reforming our desires? Sometimes Christian preaching tends in this direction. Sometimes it is said that if we have stored our treasures in heaven, no earthly suffering can harm us. Genuine faith brings true happiness, it is said.

I think the matter is more complicated. Yes, Christian doctrine teaches us to redirect our desires; but no, we cannot eliminate the *eudaimonia* gap; instead, in important ways Christianity intensifies the gap. In particular, Christianity makes us more aware of the "positive side" of the *eudaimonia* gap, and for that reason Christianity makes hope a central virtue for people on the way. I'll say more about this in a bit.

Martha Nussbaum sides with Aristotle against the Platonist and Stoic answers to the *eudaimonia* gap.[7] Human nature is both "erotic," because we desire things (all kinds of things, not just sex), and "rational," because we can learn how the world works. On Aristotle's view, *eudaimonia* is a state to be found in this world, not some transcendent realm of the forms; it is experienced when rational persons enjoy reasonable fulfillment of their desires. But this good life is *fragile*, subject to luck. As Nussbaum sees it, the Platonist and Stoic positions try to create a kind of invulnerability for the wise person. *Tuchê* no longer threatens the philosopher who has seen the forms (Plato) or lives in accord with *logos* (Zeno). Against these views, Nussbaum asks: Would "we" really be "us" if we changed our desires to such a degree? Would we still recognize ourselves as human beings, if the ordinary dreams listed by my students (travel, relationships, career, etc.) mattered little to us? Nussbaum doesn't discuss Epicureanism, Christianity (of the "world is not my home" variety), or Buddhism, but her criticism of Plato may be turned against these advices too. In general: if the answer to the *eudaimonia* gap is that we should change our desires—and change them drastically, so that we are invulnerable to chance—would we

7. Nussbaum, *Fragility of Goodness*, 318–72.

be saving our lives or would we be making ourselves into something else, perhaps angels or aliens?

Rather than trimming our desires, the second response to the *eudaimonia* gap says we should hold onto many of our desires. Recognizing we do not have what we desire, we live in hope. There are two ways this can be done.

Embracing the Gap: Tragic Hope

The Platonist and the Stoic say we can protect ourselves against *tuchê* by means of a right philosophy. A Christian of the "this world is not my home" variety says we can be saved, no matter what our earthly misfortune, by means of faith.[8] A Buddhist says bad luck cannot harm the one who through right mindfulness has achieved enlightenment.

Against all such views, Martha Nussbaum approves an image from the Greek poet Pindar. Human excellence "is like a young plant: something growing in the world, slender, fragile, in constant need of food from without."[9] Sometimes *tuchê* threatens our good lives from outside us, by war, disease, etc. But other times bad luck arises within the soul, as when human passion—the heights of love, without which Nussbaum thinks we would not be fully human—makes us vulnerable to betrayal and desire for revenge.

In Nussbaum's world, the best we can do is the best we can do. There is no rational plan, no philosophy, that can fully guard us against *tuchê*. We must be open to the possibility of tragedy. The "young plant" which is our life *may* grow and flourish, and wise persons will seek to nurture human excellence in themselves and their societies. But there is no promise we will succeed.

To invent a term, we could call Nussbaum's advice *tragic hope*. On this view, a rational person can have genuine hope. That is, she can see that the good life she desires is possible, and she may be able to act in ways that increase the likelihood of good outcomes. As long as the particular goods she desires are possible, she may continue to hope. Rather than trimming her hope, she can cling to it and it may sustain her through many hardships. But tragic hope is always vulnerable to *tuchê*. If and when happenstance makes

8. Historically, dualistic Christianity draws as much from the well of Platonism as it does from the Bible. One might say that very often in church history Christians have read scripture through the lenses of their Plato glasses.

9. Nussbaum, *Fragility of Goodness*, 1.

the object-states we desire impossible, tragic hope dies. (And any hope that ignores the finality of death is irrational, not genuine hope.) We can say that tragic hope *embraces* the gap. The knowledge that the goods we desire are subject to luck embellishes tragic hope with a kind of beauty.

Living in the Gap: Kingdom Hope

Christian hope is rooted in God's promises for the future. Unfortunately, a great many people, including very many Christians, are uninformed or positively misinformed about what God's promises are. Fortunately, N. T. Wright and other scholars have done much to accurately explain New Testament Christian beliefs about the future.[10] I will discuss the content of Christian hope with more detail in chapters 7 and 8. For now, summary comments will suffice.

First, Christian hope is *not* only about going to heaven. Jesus' preaching centered on the kingdom of God. He urged people to repent because the kingdom was breaking in, taking form in and through Jesus' own ministry. Jesus taught his disciples to pray for God's kingdom to come, for God's will to be done on earth. Any understanding of Christian hope that reduces Christian hope to the thought of "flying away" with Jesus leaves out much of what we are to hope for.

Second, the doctrine of resurrection is essential to Christian hope. First-century Christians believed that Jesus was raised from the dead, a fact of history, and that God would also raise all Jesus' followers in the future. This means that Christian hope can never be tragic hope; no matter how many times or how badly our hopes are frustrated in this life, we have reason to hope for eventual triumph.

In a sense, Christian hope does "trim" our desires. Raw human beings—that is, people as we see them every day, including Christians—hold many unreasonable and sometimes evil desires. We should only hope for object-states that accord with the values of the kingdom of God. But since the kingdom is to come on earth, many of our hopes should be earthly hopes.

---

10. See Wright, *Surprised by Hope*. Wright is particularly concerned to explain first-century Christian thinking. Elliot's *Hope and Christian Ethics* focuses on Thomas Aquinas's treatment of hope from the thirteenth century. Christians of the twenty-first century should learn from both.

Christian hope lives *in* the *eudaimonia* gap. Because Christians hope for nothing less than the kingdom of God, they should be more intensely aware of the gap between the lives we live now and the good lives we desire. At the same time, because Christian hope is rooted in the triumph of Jesus, it can never be tragic hope.

Two Twenty-First-Century Hopes

Historical "location" matters. For example, as a Christian praying in the 1980s for God's kingdom to come on earth, I prayed for peaceful change in the Soviet Union. My prayers grew out of, and partially constituted, *hope* for peaceful change in world affairs. Believers in earlier centuries would have prayed in general terms for God's sovereign reign over the nations, but obviously they didn't pray about the Soviet Union. The details of our hopes respond to the specifics of our historical situation.

The beginning of the twenty-first century brings two illustrations of the "positive side" of the *eudaimonia* gap unknown to prior generations. It is morally right for people in our time to hope for these things as long as they remain possible.

First, we should hope to avoid world war. Human history has always been stained by collective organized violence, the wars of tribe against tribe, nation against nation, empire against empire. In the twentieth century, industry and technology brought us to a new level in our ability to slaughter one another. Thermonuclear weapons, if used on a large scale, would probably kill all of us and would certainly end civilization. For more than seventy years, the fear of mutually assured destruction has helped steer world leaders away from "major power" wars, but it has not stopped scientific and technological production of new weapons. Biologically engineered weapons (which may already exist, under cover of bureaucratic secrecy) could threaten whole populations. And in an increasingly wired world, cyber warfare could wreak havoc on production and control systems everywhere. In short: though human beings continue to kill each other in collective organized violence, we have for seven decades refrained from using our worst weapons, though we continue to invent new ones. As I noted in chapter 1, sometimes hope is the reverse side of fear; it is obviously rational and morally right to hope that we avoid world war. Even persons who do not hope for worldwide peace (perhaps approving a limited war to achieve certain ends) ought to hope that we avoid world war.

Second, we ought to hope to end absolute poverty. I rely here on a distinction between relative poverty and absolute poverty. *Relative poverty* is comparative. One person or group is judged "poor" because some other person or group has greater wealth. Compared to the majority of the world's people, most Americans are not poor, but they may think themselves poor if they compare themselves to the richest fifth of our population. I do not deny that relative poverty is an important issue socially and politically in many countries. It may be morally important to reduce relative poverty.[11]

Absolute poverty (or extreme poverty) is poverty that threatens the minimum goods all people should have. For most of human history a large percentage of the human population has lived within one bad harvest of starvation. History books are full of kings and princes, priests and prophets, poets and warriors—but for thousands of years most of our ancestors were peasants who farmed, hunted, or fished at a subsistence level.

In the last four centuries the picture changed dramatically. World population rose from a few hundred million people in the 1600s (less in ancient times) to 1 billion around 1800, 3 billion in 1960, to more than 7 billion today. In spite of this enormous growth in population, worldwide economic growth was even greater. Some economists estimate that perhaps 1 billion of the world's people still live in absolute poverty. The rest live at some level of prosperity.[12]

Economists point to multiple overlapping factors that created this new situation: science and technology; trade via ships, railroads, airplanes, and modern roads; widespread education; immunizations and other healthcare improvements; the Industrial Revolution; the Green Revolution in agriculture, and so on. These sweeping and interlocking changes have brought political, social, and religious turmoil to every corner of the world. But the economic bottom line should not be missed: whereas historically most

---

11. Consider a mental experiment. Hypothetically, we will say "Bill Gates" is the richest American. (For all I know this might have been true of the real Mr. Gates in the 1990s. It is not true now, in 2021.) "Bill Gates" is far richer than me. When the stock market takes a downturn, as it did when the dot.com bubble burst in 2001 or when the recession hit in 2008, Gates lost many times as much wealth as I did. At those times my "relative poverty," measured against Bill Gates, was greatly reduced. Should we regard this reduction in inequality as a good thing? I think not. My point here is related to John Rawls's difference principle: social and political changes should be judged by whether they benefit those who get less; if the conditions of the person at the bottom of the heap are improved by some change, it does not matter if persons higher on the economic scale benefit even more. Reductions in relative poverty may or may not help the poor.

12. Sachs, *End of Poverty*, 18.

human beings lived in absolute poverty, today a shrinking minority of our fellow human beings live in absolute poverty. For the first time in our history, it is possible that in this century we could end absolute poverty.[13]

It seems obvious (to me at least) that people of good will—certainly followers of Jesus—ought to hope for the end of absolute poverty. When we pray for the kingdom of God to come on earth, this is one of the particulars we should have in mind.

Summary

Everyone needs hope, because we all experience the *eudaimonia* gap. We find our lives subject to *tuchê*, and hope can help us persist in our pursuit of genuinely good object-states. Rather than trim our hopes to protect ourselves against luck, Martha Nussbuam advises that we acknowledge the fragility of our hopes ("tragic" hope). As a Christian, I advise that we hope for the kingdom of God, both in ultimate enjoyment of friendship with God and the achievement of godly object-states in this life. Some of these object-states will be "small"; we hope for better lives for ourselves and our families. But some appropriate object-states are "big"; we hope for an end to poverty and an avoidance of world war.

---

13. Sachs, *End of Poverty*, 1.

3

Is Hope a Good Thing?

I n *Man's Search for Meaning*, psychiatrist Viktor Frankl reflected on his experiences in a Nazi prison camp in World War II:

> As we said before, any attempt to restore a man's inner strength in the camp had first to succeed in showing him some future goal. Nietzsche's words, "He who has a *why* to live can bear with almost any *how*," could be the guiding motto for all psychotherapeutic and psychohygenic efforts regarding prisoners.[1]

Pretty obviously, Frankl would answer this chapter's title question affirmatively. Hope is a good thing. In the prison camps, prisoners who lost hope usually died quickly. Having a future goal not only contributed to a man's physical survival; it contributed to his inner, psychic life. Frankl writes admiringly of men who did not survive but who displayed fortitude and kindness because of their hope. In Frankl's book, the "search for meaning" is almost synonymous with a "search for hope."

The prisoners' hopes were not all the same. Frankl thought often of his wife, imagining her face and words, looking forward to the day when he might see her again. He also thought of his lost research manuscript, making notes on scraps of paper so that he could rewrite his book after the war. Naturally, other men had other future goals: to go home or some other significant place, to find a wife or child, to resume a business, to enjoy a meal, to finish an important project, and so on.

Man's Search for Meaning is a famous tribute to hope. Surely no one would disagree.

Not so fast. There are charges to be made against hope. We can start with some worries expressed by environmentalists.

1. Frankl, *Man's Search for Meaning*, 84 (italics original).

The Case against Hope

A 2016 book, *Ecology, Ethics, and Hope*, edited by Andrew Brei, contains essays by nine environmental philosophers.[2] Collectively, the authors aren't sure what to say about hope. They write in the conviction that global climate change is a fact, caused by human activity (mostly burning fossil fuels), and inevitably worsening. Far-reaching changes in human behavior might reduce the severity of climate change, but the authors think such changes are unlikely, given political and economic reality. We have entered, they say, a new geological age, the *anthropocene*, in which the activity of one species determines the environmental conditions for all other species. The authors declare that climate change, caused by human release of carbon dioxide, will be an existential threat to civilization in the current century. Global catastrophe is upon us, and only extreme and immediate changes could mitigate the crisis. It is a moral imperative that individuals and governments make those changes.

Having agreed on all the claims of the preceding paragraph, Brei and his contributors agonize about hope. They fear two possibilities. On one hand, if people think nothing effective can be done to mitigate climate change, they will *despair* and do nothing to reduce greenhouse gas emissions. Even worse, despairing people might destroy the environment faster, in order to enjoy certain pleasures. (Why not buy a gas-guzzler if I can afford it? The climate is ruined anyway.)

On the other hand, people may believe there is no climate change danger. For example, some prominent politicians say climate change science is just a hoax to destroy the coal industry. Or people may trust that a technological breakthrough will solve the problem before catastrophe changes the world. For instance, some believe carbon capture technology, once it becomes economically viable, will reverse climate change. Rather than despair, these people exhibit blind *optimism*. They probably will do nothing, either in their personal or political lives, to combat climate change.

Both possibilities, despair and optimism, alarm Brei's writers. *Hope* is often praised as something that sustains people in hard times. The environmental ethicists want to praise it too. We certainly have hard work to do to ward off the worst effects of climate change. Hope can guard against despair; in the hard fight against climate disaster, we might even say people have a duty to hope. But very often hope is equated with optimism. And

2. Brei, *Ecology, Ethics, and Hope*.

that is what we must not do, say the environmental ethicists. Our situation is dire, they insist. We need hope rather than despair, but we must not let our hope be mere optimism. Both despair and optimism will tear us away from the hard work we need to do.

We can sum up the ambivalence of the environmental ethicists toward hope this way. *Hope may be a good thing, but we need to get it right.*

Perhaps no one will object to that, but many will ask what it means to "get it right." How should we understand hope so that we do not fall into either despair or blind optimism?

Before we answer the question, let's sharpen it. Let's listen to Simon Critchley and Friedrich Nietzsche, who—along with other modern philosophers—are skeptical about hope.

In April 2014, Critchley wrote an essay for *The Stone*, one of the opinion pages for the *New York Times*, entitled "Abandon (Nearly) All Hope," that captures the modern philosophers' objection to hope.[3] Writing at Eastertime, Critchley meditated on the dangers of Barack Obama's campaign theme, "audacious hope." Obama picked up the phrase from his pastor, Jeremiah Wright Jr., and said that this audacity is "the best of the American spirit." It is "the audacity to believe despite all the evidence to the contrary."[4] If that's what hope is, Critchley thinks it's dangerous, a vice rather than a virtue.

Political decisions based on hope rather than realism can lead to disaster. Critchley reminds us of Thucydides's account of the Melians, when besieged by the Athenians. The Athenian army was clearly stronger, and the Athenian navy controlled the waters around Melos. Still, the Melians hoped: they hoped they might hold out for a long time, they hoped their allies, the Spartans, would come to relieve them, and they hoped to win honor for standing against oppression. Acting on the basis of hope, the Melians refused to surrender. Their patience exhausted, the Athenians conquered the city, killed all the men, and made slaves of the women and children. Critchley says:

> Thucydides offers no moral commentary on the Melian Dialogue. He does not tell us how to react, but instead impartially presents us with a real situation. The dialogue is an argument from power about the nature of power. This is why Nietzsche, in his polemics against Christianity and liberalism, loved Thucydides. This is also

3. Critchley, "Abandon (Nearly) All Hope."
4. Critchley, "Abandon (Nearly) All Hope," para. 6.

why I love Nietzsche. Should one reproach Thucydides for describing the negotiations between the Athenians and the Melians
without immediately moralizing the story and telling us how we
should think? Not at all, Nietzsche insists. What we witness in the
Melian Dialogue is the true character of Greek *realism*.[5]

Here is the heart of the attack on hope. *When it is unrealistic, hope can
(and often does) make our lives worse.* The environmental ethicists worry
that hope, misunderstood as optimism, will make our climate catastrophe
worse. If in regard to climate change our hope is that carbon capture technology or some other technological breakthrough will magically save the
day, we may let ourselves off the hard tasks that need doing.

Critchley applied the lesson to politics, thinking in particular (in
2014) about Obama's policies toward the Middle East. But his warning can
be easily applied to many other hopes, both in public policy and individual
lives. Imagine the tragedies people make of their lives by "audacious hope"
in regard to gambling, investments, business decisions, or relationships.
Against all evidence to the contrary, they hope that *this* horse will win, *this*
penny stock will prosper, *this* business partner will have integrity, or *this*
romantic partner will understand me. Think of the suffering resulting from
city or county decisions to approve risky land uses, while hoping that the
worst would not happen. In Japan, a tsunami floods a nuclear power plant.
In America, rusting pipes poison a city's water with lead.

Now hopefulness is a positive emotion. It feels good; no one denies
that. For that reason, it is all the more dangerous, Critchley would say.
When we act on the basis of hope rather than realism, we court catastrophe.
Then, when catastrophe comes, we feel despair. It's not only that a bad feeling, despair, replaces a good feeling, optimism. In many cases the disaster
created by audacious hope leaves us objectively worse off.

Critchley concludes his essay with criticism of politically liberal ideal-
ism, but his words apply equally well to many other hopes, including individual hopes:

> You can have all kinds of reasonable hopes, it seems to me, the
> kind of modest, pragmatic and indeed deliberately fuzzy concep-
> tion of social hope expressed by an anti-Platonist philosopher like
> Richard Rorty. But unless those hopes are realistic we will end up
> in a blindly hopeful (and therefore hopeless) idealism. Prodigal
> hope invites despair only when we see it fail. In giving up the

5. Critchley, "Abandon (Nearly) All Hope," para. 16.

former, we might also avoid the latter. This is not an easy task, I know. But we should try. Nietzsche writes, "Hope is the evil of evils because it prolongs man's torment." Often, by clinging to hope, we make the suffering worse.[6]

We can sharpen Critchley's point. If hope, whether we call it "audacious" or not, leads us to act in ways that often make our lives objectively worse, hope is not a virtue. Only reasonable hopes count as virtues. *In many cases, hope is not reasonable, and when it is not reasonable, hope is a vice.*[7]

Critchley and Nietzsche picture the contest as one between hope and realism, and they come down on the side of realism. If they had used an older term from the virtue tradition, they might have opposed hope to "prudence," the old-fashioned translation of *phronêsis* (usually rendered nowadays as "practical wisdom"). Aristotle counted *phronêsis* as a crucially important virtue, since a person needs it to rightly practice courage, generosity, friendship, or any other moral virtue. But Aristotle said nothing about hope as a virtue; hope enters the virtue tradition through Christianity. So here is another way to conceptualize the attack on hope. If hope is to be counted a moral virtue, it should be governed by prudence (*phronêsis*, practical wisdom). Since "audacious hope" runs free of prudence, Critchley might say, it is no more a virtue than the so-called "courage" of the foolhardy soldier who races toward the enemy forces alone.

Critchley's attack on hope doesn't have to condemn all hope. Hope is only bad, the objector could say, when it leads us to make foolish decisions. If we circumscribe our hopes so that we hope only in accord with the probability of the outcomes we desire, hope ceases to be so dangerous. "Audacious" hope is a vice, but tamed and reasonable hope could be a virtue, though a minor one.

But if hope is only a minor virtue, a different problem arises. Andrew Brei and the environmental ethicists might ask whether a tamed, domesticated hope will be sufficient to the hard tasks ahead of us. If we only aim at weak hopes, do we escape despair?

---

6. Critchley, "Abandon (Nearly) All Hope," para. 22.

7. Some readers will note that both Viktor Frankl and Simon Critchley quote Nietzsche, but in opposing ways. What did Nietzsche really think about hope? Would he accept it as a virtue, as Frankl does? Or did he regard it as a poisoned "gift" of the gods? I suspect Critchley's reading of Nietzsche is closer to the truth, but so much of Nietzsche's writing is aphoristic that it's hard to be sure.

How Strong Hope Can Be Rational

What I have labeled the "core definition" of hope, in chapter 1, is what Adrienne Martin calls the modern "orthodox" definition of hope: "to hope for an outcome is to desire it while believing it is possible but not certain."[8] Virtually all modern philosophers who talk about hope, from Hume to Nietzsche, would accept this definition. Since there is a wide field of probability between impossibility and certainty, "hope" thus defined names very different cases. We can hope for probable outcomes and be rewarded (usually) with satisfaction. We can hope "audaciously" and be punished (almost always) with despair.

Adrienne Martin objects to the "orthodox definition" of hope, first because it sweeps too much together under the vague term "desire." Hope is not just desire; it includes beliefs, motivations, and perceptions. As I said in chapter 1, hope is complicated. Martin borrows the word "syndrome" to express hope's complexity. The various parts of the "hope syndrome" are equivalent to the elements of a "positive causal network," to use Michael Bishop's term. I will discuss these matters in chapter 4.

Second, Martin objects that the orthodox definition of hope makes it impossible to explain the way different people respond to cases of "hoping against hope," that is, cases in which the probability of the desired outcome is very low. Critchley based his attack on hope on just such cases. Audacious hope is bad, Critchley argued, precisely because the desired outcome is unlikely. Martin objects: before we can judge whether hope is good or bad, we must see whether the proposed definition (what she calls the "orthodox" definition and I have called the "core definition") is accurate.

If hope is simply desire for some outcome combined with the belief that the outcome is possible, why is it that people who have the same desire for an outcome and the same belief about its likelihood can have very different levels of hope?[9] The defender of the orthodox definition might suggest that the person with greater hope somehow has stronger desires for the good outcome or surreptitiously assigns a higher probability to it. Martin gives good reasons to suppose these answers are insufficient.

Consider two terminal cancer patients, Alan and Bess.[10] Their doctors approach them with an opportunity to try an experimental drug. The

8. Martin, *How We Hope*, 5.

9. Martin, *How We Hope*, 11–17.

10. Martin, *How We Hope*, 13–14.

doctors think the new drug has perhaps a 1-in-10,000 chance of curing them; they explain to Alan and Bess that the doctors' real interest in offering the drug is gaining research data.

Alan and Bess both recognize that the experimental drug offered to them has an extremely low chance of success. But Alan hopes only a little or not at all, while Bess hopes strongly. How should we explain the difference between them? Is Bess somehow deceiving herself about the odds? Does Bess desire life more than Alan? Even if one of these options could explain a particular case, would this be true in every case? Martin points to an experience that many people have shared: over a period of time, perhaps a single day, our subjective sense of the probability of some event may change without strengthening or weakening our hope for that event. Hope seems to be something much more complicated than the formula: desire + probability judgment = hope. Martin concludes that hope cannot be adequately captured in the orthodox definition.

Martin offers her "incorporation analysis" as alternative to the orthodox definition. We need to see that there are *two* judgments made by the person who hopes. In the cancer case, Bess does not deceive herself into thinking the drug has a greater chance of success. Hope is not the same as wishful thinking. When we estimate the likelihood that our desired outcomes will occur, Martin says we ought to make our judgments in accord with ordinary standards of reason and evidence. However, the fact that the desired outcome is improbable does not imply that one cannot hope for it. Instead, the person who hopes then makes a second, practical, judgment. The person who hopes sees that the desired outcome is *important* to her. On the basis of these two judgments—that the desired outcome is possible, and that it is important—the person who hopes "licenses" herself to build a syndrome of hope. Thus, Martin says that hoping for an outcome has four parts:

1. Be attracted to the outcome in virtue of certain of its features;

2. Assign a probability between and exclusive of 0 and 1 to the outcome;

3. Adopt a stance toward that probability whereby it licenses treating one's attraction to the outcome (and the outcome's attractive features) as a reason for certain ways of thinking, feeling, and/or planning with regard to the hoped-for outcome; and

4. Treat one's attraction and the outcome's attractive features as sufficient reason for those ways of thinking, feeling, and/or planning.[11]

If hope is merely desire + probability judgment, as modern philosophers seem to think, then it seems the wise advice is to trim one's hopes
to fit probability. People who hope for improbable things will very likely
have their hopes squashed. We all know or ought to know this. Therefore,
people who hope for improbable things most likely are simply deceiving
themselves. If you want to avoid the crushing disappointment of dashed
hopes, don't deceive yourself. Don't get your hopes up.

Simon Critchley says we should limit our hopes to those that are
realistic. Against such so-called "realism," Martin's incorporation analysis
says that hope can be rational even when the probability of the hoped-for
outcome is very small. Martin invites us to consider the fictional Andy
Dufresne, in *The Shawshank Redemption*.[12] Andy and his friend, Red, are
convicts in the Shawshank prison. Red warns Andy explicitly against the
dangers of hope. "Let me tell you something, my friend. Hope is a dangerous thing. Hope can drive a man insane."[13] If you hope, you get crushed.
Red's advice mirrors the advice of modern philosophers like Critchley.
Against Red's advice, Andy hopes to escape from prison.

Notice: Andy's hope is entirely consistent with a belief that successful
escape is very unlikely. Martin insists that hopeful people must judge the
probability of their desired outcomes by ordinary standards of reason and
evidence. This is Martin's point 2.

But Andy's thought process goes further, to a second judgment. He
recognizes that his hoped-for escape is a very important goal; in Martin's
words, he decides that his "attraction to the outcome (and the outcome's
attractive features)" is "a reason for certain ways of thinking, feeling, and/
or planning." This is Martin's point 3.

The first judgment, a judgment of probability, is governed by ordinary
standards of reason and evidence. The second judgment, a licensing judgment, is governed by standards of *practical* rationality. Practical judgments
must take into account a person's moral obligations, projects, relationships,
abilities, and so on. Given Andy's situation—a life sentence for a crime he
did not commit—the very low probability of escape can still function as
organizing grounds for his hope. He entertains certain *thoughts*. He lets

11. Martin, *How We Hope*, 62.

12. Martin, *How We Hope*, 15–16.

13. Darabont, *Shawshank Redemption*, 1:12:18–1:12:40.

himself feel certain *feelings*. He *imagines* certain future scenes. He plans and executes certain *actions*. In the movie, Andy eventually escapes. But the value of hope does not depend on this happy outcome. Andy's hope sustained him through many years of imprisonment, and he would have enjoyed this benefit even if his escape failed in the end. The moral of the story is expressed in Andy's words to Red: "Remember, Red, hope is a good thing. Maybe the best thing, and no good thing ever dies."[14]

Summarized and paraphrased, Martin's position is something like this: *hope, understood as an incorporation of a syndrome of thoughts, feelings, perceptions, and motivations into one's life, can be rational, even in cases when the hoped-for outcome is very unlikely.*

Critchley's criticism of audacious hope focused on political examples. Martin's argument depends on individual cases. Can her defense of hope's rationality be extended to politics?

Yes. Consider the hopes of Palestinians living in the West Bank and Gaza. They want to live in a peaceful independent state, with secure land rights and human dignity. Very often, "realism" teaches that these dreams are unlikely. Israeli occupation of the West Bank seems permanent. Martin's analysis suggests that such people may still hope. Without deluding themselves about the likelihood of a secure independent state, they may incorporate hope for such a state into their lives. In point of fact, many Palestinian people find such hope to be a crucial part of their lives. It sustains them through generations of occupation.

Israelis also have room for hope, focusing on peaceful relations with Muslim neighbors. However unlikely a secure peace may appear, they may judge such an object-state to be important enough to dream about it and pursue it.

Of course, some instances of "hope" fail to be rational. If a person allows his desire for a certain outcome to skew his estimation of its probability (the first judgment), his hope would be irrational. Probability judgments must be made according to ordinary standards of reason and evidence. It is also possible that a person could misjudge the practical importance of some desired outcome (the second judgment); this would produce another kind of irrational "hope."

Silly illustration #1: Ben is a Cubs fan. On September 12, he reads that the Cubs are "only" twelve games from first place. The Cubs played well last night, so Ben estimates that the Cubs will probably play well in their

14. Darabont, *Shawshank Redemption*, 2:15:45–2:15:55.

remaining games, therefore he licenses himself to hope for a Cubs pennant. This estimation of probability violates ordinary standards of reason and evidence. (For nonbaseball fans: the odds of any team twelve games from first in mid-September winning the pennant are astronomically improbable.)

Martin says that people who hope for very improbable things frequently have backup plans. "Hope for the best, plan for the worst."[15] Bess hopes that the experimental drug will cure her cancer, but hoping does not mean she deceives herself about the probable outcome. She may well make plans for her death (e.g., preparing a will, buying a burial niche, etc.). Similarly, in the Shawshank case, Andy's hope does not mean he thinks it is likely that he will escape. In the story, he writes letters for many years to ask for money for the prison library in order to improve conditions of long-term prison life for himself and other prisoners. Efforts to improve the prison library and thus improve long-term prison life coexist in his mind with actions to prepare his escape. Palestinians and Israelis who hope for peace may still plan how to endure interminable checkpoints and guard against suicide attackers.

Silly illustration #2: Pasadena resident Charley reads that there will be a partial eclipse of the sun visible in Miami on January 2. Charley is not interested in astronomy. Though he has tickets to the Rose Bowl where his beloved UCLA Bruins will play on January 1, Charley decides to fly to Miami on that day, hoping to see the eclipse. Given Charley's interests, this "hope" violates the notion that practical judgments are subject to standards of practical reason, because Charley's "hope" does not reflect anything important to him and it interferes with something that actually is important to him.

Practical judgments vary from person to person. Given the same deadly cancer and the same highly unlikely cure via the experimental drug, it may be rational for Bess to license herself to hope for a cure and equally rational for Alan to reject such hope. Practical judgments must be sensitive to the particulars of a person's life and situation. If there is such a thing as a "duty" to hope, or a "task" of hope, it would be based on overridingly important features of a person's life.

So yes: hope may be irrational. It is irrational to let our hope influence our judgment of the probability of the outcome we want. It is also irrational to let hopes for trivial outcomes play too big a role in one's life. Nevertheless,

---

15. Martin, *How We Hope*, 22.

against the "orthodox" advice, Adrienne Martin concludes that it may be—and often is—rational to hope for unlikely object-states.

Do Backup Plans Negate Hope?

Martin's defense of the rationality of hope might leave some readers feeling uneasy. Critchley's attack on hope focuses on actions. Using Martin's word, Critchley might say the Melians "licensed" themselves to hope that their Spartan allies would rescue them. But when they *acted* on that hope, by refusing the Athenians' terms for surrender, they doomed themselves. On Martin's account, people may rationally hope for improbable object-states, but they ought to have "backup plans" in case hopes are dashed. What backup plan did the Melians have? What about cases in which acting on one's hope abrogates one's backup plan?

Life sometimes presents us with either/or choices. To act one way means not acting another way. It seems that at some point to act in accord with hope will require abandoning one's backup plan. In *The Shawshank Redemption*, Andy spends thousands of hours over many years tunneling through the prison's massive walls. Meanwhile, prison life went on: he kept books for the corrupt warden's fraudulent schemes and wrote letters to the prison governing board asking for improvements to the prison library. But there came a time when he had to act decisively. When Andy made his break for freedom all his backup plans fell to the ground. Either he would achieve his desired object-state, or he would be captured and probably killed.

Martin cites the proverb: "Hope for the best and prepare for the worst." Critchley could respond: "You can't have it both ways. Sometimes hope undermines wise preparation." How should we settle this dispute?

First, we should say that very often we *can* have both. It is no contradiction for Bess to hope the experimental drug will cure her while also arranging for her burial. Forced-choice situations do occur, but nonforced-choice situations are also real. If one's plans to achieve her desired object-state do not interfere with backup plans, there is nothing wrong with planning for that object-state. Martin could concede that in forced-choice situations we should act in accord with prudence and still maintain that in many cases hope for unlikely outcomes can be rational.

Second, actions and plans for action are parts of the syndrome analysis of hope, but only parts. Hope includes perceptions, beliefs, and feelings. A person's hope for a certain object-state may be very important and helpful to him even when he can do nothing to achieve that object-state. I will say more about *hoping as waiting* in chapter 7.

Third, it is possible that the practical importance of one's desired object-state is so great that it outweighs the cost of a highly probable bad outcome. One might be forced to choose between a safe course of action leading to a very likely outcome and a risky course leading to a desired but very unlikely outcome. In such a case it is not always irrational to take the risk, hoping for something wonderful.

Philip Hallie and Realistic Hope

In the preface to his book, *Lest Innocent Blood be Shed*, Philip Hallie wrote:

> I am a student and teacher of good and evil, but for me ethics, like the rest of philosophy, is not a scientific, impersonal matter. It is by and about persons, much as it was for Socrates. Being personal, it must not be ashamed to express personal passions, the way a strict scientist might be ashamed to express them in a laboratory report. My own passion was a yearning for realistic hope. I wanted to believe that the examined life was more precious than this Hell I had dug for myself in studying evil.[16]

Philip Hallie, an American Jew, served as an artillery gunner in the US army in 1944–45. He experienced battlefield horrors firsthand, frozen body parts lying like cordwood in German forests. Studying philosophy after the war, he became a holocaust expert, studying the Nazi extermination of Jews and others in excruciating detail. The more he learned, the darker his private hell became. The Nazi evil was horrible and at the same time banal and boring: story after story of brutality and indifference. Was overwhelming force the only answer? If in response to evil we trust in overwhelming force, what kind of future will we have? Are we trapped between death camps on one hand and nuclear winter on the other?

Then Hallie came upon a few documents that told a different story. In the village of Le Chambon, in the mountains of southern France, a community of farmers sheltered refugees during the war. Mostly Jews and mostly children, several thousand came to Le Chambon in the years 1940–44. None of them were turned away. Not all were saved: The Nazis

16. Hallie, *Lest Innocent Blood Be Shed*, 7–8.

took some of the village leaders, including a few refugees, and they were killed. But the vast majority survived.[17]

It is estimated that in Le Chambon, 5,000 Christians saved 5,000 Jews. Unlike millions of Europeans who stood by in fear or indifference during the Holocaust, these people acted. In the nature of the case, they acted mostly in secret. Hallie points out that war makes heroes of leaders like Charles de Gaulle, who make speeches and lead armies. In Le Chambon, resistance was a house-by-house operation, a kitchen rebellion with decisions often made by housewives.

The villagers were led by the pastor of a protestant church in Le Chambon, Andre Trocme. Trocme preached pacifism and love for everyone, the persecutor as well as the persecuted. He did not direct the rescue operation the way a military commander might command his troops. It was essential that no one know all the details, because capture and interrogation were constant possibilities.

I will say little more about Le Chambon and the goodness that happened there. Readers interested in the story should find Hallie's book and Pierre Sauvage's documentary.

Remember Hallie's confession: "My own passion was a yearning for *realistic hope*." Hallie was a Jew, not a Christian. He was a soldier, not a pacifist. His study of Le Chambon did not convert him to Christianity or pacifism. And yet he was drawn to the story of Le Chambon because it showed that a conspiracy of goodness had happened. Even in the extreme situation of France in 1940 (the war lost, Britain seeming certain to be defeated, Petain as Prime Minister of France), people could resist evil without adopting the methods of evil. If goodness could happen in Le Chambon in the 1940s, goodness might happen in other places, at other times.

Imagine Nietzsche or Simon Critchley transported in time to Pastor Trocme's study or—better—to a farmhouse kitchen in the countryside around Le Chambon in the winter of 1941. "What are you preparing to do?" the hope skeptic might ask. "By taking in these strangers you expose the whole village, perhaps the whole region, to Nazi reprisals. What are the chances you will succeed? Hope must be realistic. Perhaps Churchill will get the Americans to join the war. If the tide turns against Germany, that would be the time to resist."

---

17. One of the children saved was Pierre Sauvage, who grew up to become a filmmaker. His documentary, *Weapons of the Spirit*, tells the story of Le Chambon.

According to Nietzsche and Critchley, the Melians' hope led them to disaster. But it seems that Critchley's doctrine—that we should act only on modest, realistic hopes—would have prevented goodness from happening in Le Chambon.

Hallie's search for "realistic hope" provokes further reflection. If Adrienne Martin's analysis of hope is right, it can be practically rational to hope for unlikely object-states. Perhaps the story of Le Chambon shows that it can sometimes be wise to *act* on hopes for unlikely object-states, even in either/or situations in which one's "backup plan" must be abandoned. It can be wise to take the risk of hope, because without that risk great goodness will be lost (or great evil accomplished). Extreme cases, such as the story of the Melians and the story of Le Chambon, raise the possibility of transcendent hope, what Jonathan Lear calls "radical" hope, the topic of chapter 5. But before exploring radical hope, we must learn from psychologists.

4

The Psychology of Hope

S o far, we have been working with a core definition of hope (the "ortho-dox" definition, according to Adrienne Martin) that says hope combines desire for an object-state with a judgment that the object-state is possible. Martin criticizes the definition for being too simplistic, sweeping different elements of hope under the broad rubric "desire." Instead, she suggests that hope is like a syndrome, a term often used by psychologists. It's time to explore more fully what psychology has to say about hope, beginning with a theory with strong similarities to the "orthodox" definition.

Snyder's Hope Theory: Pathways Plus Motivation

"Positive psychology" is a broad movement in late twentieth- and early twen-ty-first-century psychology that moves the focus of psychology from mental illness (fixing what is wrong) to the achievement of satisfactory life (pursu-ing and enjoying what is right or healthy). Charles R. Snyder (1944–2006) wrote the first textbook in positive psychology and was a leader in the field. He spent his career as a teacher, researcher, and theorist at the University of Kansas. In the 1970s and 1980s, while conducting research on the excuses people give for failing to reach goals, Snyder theorized that excuses help people distance themselves from failures. But as he listened to his research participants, they had something more to say. Excuses were only part of the story. Yes, they wanted to distance themselves from failures, but they also wanted to *decrease the distance* to their positive life goals. Reflection on this research led Snyder to propose "hope theory."[1]

1. Snyder, *Handbook of Hope*, 5–8.

Snyder's core definition: *Hope is the sum of perceived capabilities to produce routes to desired goals, along with the perceived motivation to use those routes.*[2]

Much of human life is teleological; that is, we pursue goals. Snyder offers a simple diagram:

Protagonist (A) ➔ Goal (B).

But we often encounter obstacles that keep us from reaching our goals. This gives us a more complicated diagram.

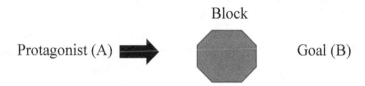

Two things are needed to reach life goals when obstacles get in the way, Snyder thought. A person needs to be able to think up "pathways" around the obstacle that may enable her to reach the goal, and she needs to have "agentic motivation" to invent these pathways and put them into practice.

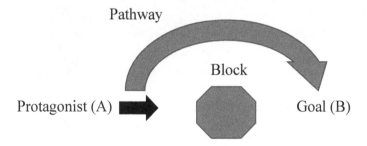

The protagonist encounters a block to the desired goal and then finds an alternative way to get the goal. The protagonist perceives herself has having both the ability to find new paths to the goal and the motivation to use such paths.

2. Snyder, *Handbook of Hope*, 8.

In the fifteen years after 1990, Snyder and his team of colleagues and students at the University of Kansas built an impressive array of research on this fundamental idea. They devised the Adult Dispositional Hope Scale, the Adult State Hope Scale, the Children's Hope Scale, the Young Children's Hope Scale, and the Adult Domain-Specific Hope Scale.[3] The scales are composed of a surprisingly small number of items, fewer than twenty in every case.[4] Testing their hope scales on a variety of populations including college students, children, adults, and senior adults, the Kansas researchers made several impressive claims: the hope scales give reliable information, comparable to other accepted psychological inventories;[5] high hope scores correlate well with positive life outcomes;[6] and therapeutic interventions can be devised to increase clients' hope.[7] Further, Snyder offered a possible explanation for a surprising but well-documented finding about psychological therapy, i.e., that various psychological approaches for producing change in clients appear to be equally effective. Therapeutic interventions based on seemingly very different psychological theories all have a common feature of offering hope to clients. Perhaps it is hope, and not the particular theoretical construct, that really matters.[8]

Snyder and his colleagues claimed that both parts of hope, *agency* and *pathways thinking*, are necessary to increase hopefulness and improve life outcomes. A client suffering from depression (or some other presenting problem) might perceive himself as being unable or without desire to do anything in regard to his goals (a lack of agency), unable to think of ways to achieve his goals (lack of pathways thinking), or both. *Hope therapy* aims to discover which deficits are present and help the client come to perceive himself as being able in both areas. Self-perception is crucial; according to hope theory, if a client sees himself as motivated and willing to use appropriate methods of achieving his goals and sees himself as able to invent appropriate methods of achieving his goals, he exhibits hope.

Snyder and his research team applied this analysis to many areas of life. The Domain-Specific Hope Scale includes social relationships,

3. Lopez et al., "Diagnosing for Strengths," 58.

4. Lopez et al., "Diagnosing for Strengths," 76–84. The Domain Specific Hope Scale uses more questions, but no more than nine in any particular domain.

5. Lopez et al., "Diagnosing for Strengths," 60.

6. Lopez et al., "Hope Therapy," 123.

7. Lopez et al., "Hope Therapy," 123–25.

8. Snyder and Taylor, "Hope as a Common Factor," 89–90.

academics, romantic relationships, family life, work, and leisure activities.[9] Hope therapy is appropriate, the hope researchers claimed, with every age group, from young children to the elderly.

Hope therapy aims at changing the way clients *think*. "In hope therapy, change is initiated at the cognitive level, with a focus on enhancing clients' self-referential agentic and pathway goal-directed thinking."[10] Snyder and his colleagues thought that affective changes—that is, changes in a client's feelings—would follow from changed thinking. This put hope theory and hope therapy in sharp contrast to much previous psychological interest in hope, which thought of hope primarily in terms of positive emotions.

Hope theory says that hope is goal-directed, but it doesn't say much about which goals are appropriate. It is the *client* who decides which areas of life are important to her and what her goals are in those areas. Therapists may have to help clients make their amorphous goals more specific, and they may actively redirect clients' thinking so they can acknowledge their own abilities to conceive of goals and pathways to them. But Snyder and his colleagues do not directly address philosophical or religious questions about which object-states we ought to desire.

I will not try to describe hope therapy in greater detail now. Suffice it to say that Snyder and his colleagues produced (and after Snyder's death his colleagues are still producing) a generous supply of research and "how-to" materials for psychological professionals.

How does hope theory as presented by Snyder and his colleagues square with the preliminary definition of hope I gave in chapter 1? I offer three observations.

First, Snyder's hope theory and the core definition (aka "orthodox" definition) are both *teleological*. Hope looks toward the future.

Second, crucial to Snyder's theory is the idea of "blocks" to goals. This matches an important feature of Thomas Aquinas's analysis of hope. According to Aquinas, human passions come in two kinds. "Concupiscent" passions move one to attain something perceived as good (e.g., hunger or sexual desire), or avoid something perceived as evil (e.g., sadness or hatred). "Irascible" passions move one to overcome some threat or difficulty that stands in the way of one's goals (e.g., courage or anger). Aquinas included hope among the irascible passions. On Aquinas's account, natural hope—that is, hope for goods in this world—is a passion that moves us to

9. Lopez et al., "Diagnosing for Strengths," 77–81.
10. Lopez et al., "Hope Therapy," 126.

attain a possible *but difficult* good. And what is true of hope as a passion is also true of theological hope, Aquinas thought. We desire nothing less than everlasting fellowship with an infinite and holy God; apart from the grace of God, this is the most difficult good imaginable. In theological hope we keep our eyes on a very high prize indeed.

Snyder's theory agrees with this insight, at least in regard to this-worldly hopes. Hope is important because it helps us overcome "blocks." Hope keeps us on track toward difficult object-states.

Third, Snyder's theory is emphatically cognitive. Snyder and his colleagues did not deny that there are feelings associated with hope, but they held that changes in affect naturally follow from cognitive change. On Snyder's account, if a person perceives himself as having motivation to use pathways to his goals and perceives himself as able to think up pathways to his goals, he exemplifies hope. If we change the way we think, we can increase hope; and if we increase hope, we can improve our lives. Snyder's "hope therapy" is intensely practical. It aims to improve patient life outcomes, and the way to do that is not to worry about our feelings but to change the way we think.

Philosophers may find this aspect of hope theory attractive. How often philosophers, from Socrates and Aristotle to the present day, have tried to identify the essential core of human nature with rationality! Philosophers might find it gratifying to discover a psychologist, someone whose task is care for souls, who emphasizes thinking rightly. But before we congratulate ourselves too much, we should ask whether Snyder's theory is too simple.

Adrienne Martin: Hope as a Syndrome

Since Aquinas, philosophers have usually defined hope as a combination of desire and a certain kind of belief. This is the "core definition" from chapter 1 and the "orthodox" definition of modern philosophers. As I explained in chapter 3, Adrienne Martin objects that the traditional definition is too simple, too easy. Borrowing language from Margaret Walker, Martin suggests that hope is a "syndrome."[11]

Consider, then, the concept of a syndrome. A syndrome is a set of medical signs and symptoms that are correlated with each other and, often, with a particular disease or disorder.[12] Notice that a syndrome may

11. Martin, *How We Hope*, 5.

12. British Medical Association (BMA), *Illustrated Medical Dictionary*, 536.

be present even if one or more of the typical symptoms is not present. Suppose a recognized syndrome was usually linked to six symptoms, a–f. One patient might display symptoms a, c, d, and e, while another patient displayed symptoms b, c, d, and f—and both would be recognized as exhibiting the same syndrome. A practical advantage of this "looseness" in describing a syndrome is that physicians or therapists will be alert to symptoms typically correlated with the disease or disorder before those symptoms show up in a particular patient.

In medicine and psychology, "syndrome" is used to describe a disease or disorder; it is a bad thing. Martin's use of the word dispenses with the negative connotation. The key idea, for Martin, is that hope is marked not just by desires and beliefs, but also by certain forms of attention, expression, feeling, and activity. One person's hope may consist in certain "symptoms" of the syndrome while another person's hope would consist in other "symptoms." The two sets of symptoms would probably overlap, but there might not be any single essential symptom. Martin criticizes Snyder's theory: "The phenomenon Snyder studies is a set of attitudes *toward one's own agency*, while hope is an attitude taken toward many outcomes and not only toward one's agency."[13]

It's clear to me that Martin is right on this point. A person may hope for many object-states that are outside her agency. For instance, she may hope that a particular candidate wins an election, that her parent's surgery goes well, or that the market price of some commodity goes up. Hope must be a much broader element of our psychology than Snyder's theory postulates.

Hope therapy, as designed by Snyder and his associates, very often helps patients live better. No mean accomplishment! Nevertheless, Snyder's theory is a map that covers only part of the territory. As I've said earlier, hope is complicated.

Michael Bishop: Hope's Place in the Good Life

Michael A. Bishop's 2015 book, *The Good Life*, introduces a philosophically informed theory of positive psychology.[14] Bishop's theory also offers insights into the virtue of hope, though Bishop probably did not intend that result.

13. Martin, *How We Hope*, 86 (italics original).
14. Bishop, *Good Life*.

Positive psychology has been a growth industry for at least forty years, reflecting the desire on the part of many mental health professionals to move from treating illness to facilitating health. The idea is intuitively appealing, at least to some. Psychologists have produced thousands of empirical studies that investigate one or more aspects of "well-being." And they have discovered correlations, some of which must represent causal connections, between behaviors, patterns of thought, accomplishments, attitudes, perceptions, and emotions. Having discovered causal connections, therapists are sometimes able to say, "Research shows that people who do x fairly reliably experience y as a result. Since you want more y in your life, I recommend you do x."

C. R. Snyder's hope theory begins with an operational definition of *hope,* and then, having conducted a great deal of empirical research on the basis of that definition, suggests practical interventions by which therapists can help patients increase their hope. As I noted above, Snyder's research colleagues have collected plenty of evidence that these interventions work, in the sense that patients report improved life outcomes on a number of measures.

It should be stressed that research into hope is only one example among many. Positive psychologists have researched organizational leadership, creativity, marital success, physical exercise, happiness, video-game playing, generosity, workplace satisfaction, and lots of other particulars.

According to Bishop, the problem is that until now no one has proposed a good theory to say what positive psychology *is.* What is it that all these empirical research programs actually study? His answer: "positive causal networks" or PCNs. Here is an illustration.

Many runners report that running improves their mood, their creativity, and their overall mental state. After much experience running, runners have a well-founded belief that goes something like this: "Even though the weather is nasty today and I'm tempted to skip my run, I know I'll feel better if I do it." This belief, or pattern of thought, obviously tends to keep the runner participating in her running regimen. There is a feedback loop: running leads to feeling better; feeling better leads to a pattern of thought; the pattern of thought leads to more running. As Bishop says, persons get "stuck" in a causal network that improves their lives.[15]

15. Bishop, *Good Life,* 35–44.

Snyder's hope theory says that a person's thinking will influence his feelings. But his theory does not explore the way changed feelings influence thinking.

Positive causal networks are usually much more complex than my example of running. Bishop lists four components to causal networks: emotions, attitudes, traits, and accomplishments. Notice that my example, running, refers to a "pattern of thought," which may seem hard to fit into one of Bishop's components. Bishop might try to squeeze "patterns of thought" into his structure (maybe such patterns contribute to "attitudes"); more likely, he would admit that the components he names may not be all there are. At several points in his book, he stresses that he is offering an initial theory and would welcome corrections. The key idea is that the parts of a positive causal network (he calls these "PCN fragments") reinforce each other.

There is plenty of evidence that positive causal networks are real, Bishop says. That is, they exist in the world whether or not we understand them or pay attention to them. To a limited degree, people have long been aware of positive causal networks, before social science began exploring them in detail. Consider the time-honored advice of parents: You say you want to do well in school? Very well, make friends with the good students. Enjoy the activities they enjoy. Copy their attitudes toward books and schoolwork. Build more friendships based on shared academic interests. And so on. Your friendships will help you develop the right attitudes and habits, the right attitudes and habits will help you do well in school, and doing well in school will attract the right kind of friends.

Bishop says we should see a parallel here between positive causal networks and other natural kinds, such as "water." Obviously, water was an important real thing in the world, though people used it and referred to it for thousands of years without knowing its chemical composition. When chemists discovered that water is H_2O, they improved our understanding of water and enabled us to do things with water that we were previously unable to do. Bishop says that as psychologists gain better understanding of positive causal networks, they will enable us to improve our lives in various ways.

One more example: people who are kind, generous, and considerate of others' feelings tend to make friends. Having friends tends to create pleasurable experiences. Having friends is a kind of personal relationship that is highly valued in our society. Having pleasurable experiences that are at the same time highly valued by society tends to make persons kind, generous, and considerate of others' feelings—and the cycle renews itself. Bishop says that much empirical research by positive psychologists supports the conclusion that PCNs are "homeostatic property clusters."[16] The emotions, traits, attitudes, and accomplishments in such a property cluster tend to reinforce each other, so the cluster tends to endure. Bishop points to empirical research that indicates that people displaying a high degree of a positive trait, attitude, emotion, or accomplishment at time t_1 will have (compared to those who have a lower degree of that trait, attitude, emotion, or accomplishment) a statistically significant greater chance of having a high degree of that trait, attitude, emotion, or accomplishment at time t_2—*even when t_2 is years or decades after t_1*. Further, persons who have a higher degree of one component of a PCN at time t_1, say component c_1, will have a greater chance of having some *other* component of the PCN, component c_2, at time t_2. Positive causal networks are real and, as homeostatic property clusters, they tend to endure. Positive psychology research can teach us how to build and strengthen PCNs. According to Bishop, that's what positive psychologists *are* doing, and that's how they *should* conceptualize their work.

Using Bishop's analysis, we might say that Snyder's hope theory has discovered parts of the homeostatic property cluster, hope. Snyder's team has discovered that changes in one element of the cluster, a person's beliefs about her ability to think up pathways and her motivation to use those pathways, will produce changes in other elements of the cluster fairly reliably.

Bishop has more to say about PCNs, PCN fragments, and the various ways PCN fragments contribute to the creation, maintenance, and strengthening of PCNs. I'm going to pass over all that. Bishop's theory does not rise or fall on such details. He would welcome corrections. Nor am I going to discuss what will undoubtedly be the most controversial thesis in his book, i.e., that "positive" causal networks are any homeostatic property clusters marked by states that feel good, are productive of states that feel good, and are valued by the agent or the agent's culture.[17] Bishop knows full well that philosophers will take him to task on this point. That a person or culture *values* a state does not mean that state is *valuable*, they will say. That a state *feels good* and leads to states that feel good does not imply *well-being*, they will say.[18] Obviously, there are fundamental questions of moral philosophy here.

16. Bishop, *Good Life*, 40.

17. Bishop, *Good Life*, 41.

18. Bishop himself gives the example of "Josef," a guard at a prison camp run by some

I will reserve those questions for another time. In this chapter I want to explore something else. What does Bishop's theory tell us about *hope*?

Bishop doesn't talk about hope very much, but when he does mention it, he uses it as an example of an "attitude."[19] Remember, attitudes are one of four elements of positive causal networks. The others are feelings (Bishop sometimes uses "moods" or "emotions"), traits, and accomplishments. I think we are to understand these categories something like this. Feelings *happen to* us. Attitudes are something we *take up* toward the world and people. And we *live out* our traits through dependable habits. Bishop doesn't make these distinctions explicitly, but I think I'm being fair to his intent.

By using hope as an example of an "attitude," Bishop treats hope far too simplistically. It is true that sometimes we willfully adopt a hopeful attitude; in this sense hope reflects our agency. But hope is also sometimes a positive feeling, something that happens to us whether we will it or not. According to Aquinas and other philosophers, there is a belief component to hope (i.e., we believe the object-state we desire is possible). And in the Christian tradition hope is a *virtue*, something we develop through habituation and that "perfects" us, in that it helps us become what we should be.

Bishop's "positive traits" are what we normally call virtues. He gives friendliness, curiosity, and perseverance as examples. But he gives no attention to the traditional idea that hope is a virtue. He seems to think of hope exclusively as hopefulness—a feeling.

Most likely, Bishop mentioned hope only to illustrate the category "positive attitudes." His attention is on positive causal networks and the things that go into them. He's not trying to give thorough analysis of hope. This is both understandable and unfortunate, because I think hope serves as an excellent illustration of his positive causal network theory. That is, hope is not just an attitude but a causal network whose parts form a homeostatic property cluster. As with Adrienne Martin's "syndrome," the "property cluster" we call hope may include desires, beliefs, forms of attention, typical forms of expression, feelings, and/or activities.

Imagine Jack. Jack has significant ambitions; he wants to begin a new career that will enable him to better provide for his family. Because of religious discrimination in his country, even though Jack is university

---

totalitarian government. Josef's society approves of his work, and Josef gets pleasure from brutalizing camp inmates. On Bishop's terms, Josef experiences well-being, a *positive* causal network. Bishop argues that we need to distinguish well-being from moral goodness. Josef experiences well-being; he just doesn't deserve it (Bishop, *Good Life*, 28).

19. Bishop, *Good Life*, 7.

educated, most occupations are closed to him in that country. Jack has a daughter who suffers from renal disease, and his neighbors tell Jack that God is punishing him for his religious errors. Medical care for his daughter is expensive and very hard to obtain.

Jack is unique, but he is not unusual. Many people face harsh obstacles in life.

Suppose that in spite of the difficulties in his life Jack is hopeful. We can think of this as an attitude that Jack adopts as an act of will. This seems to be the way Bishop thinks of hope. But how does Jack's hopeful attitude play out in his life?

One aspect of Jack's hope is that he imagines ways he could move toward his goals. C. R. Snyder called this "pathways thinking," a crucial element in Snyder's hope theory. In addition to imagining pathways, Jack makes plans on the basis of his ideas and acts on them. Sometimes, perhaps infrequently, his actions succeed; they move him toward his goals of better employment or healthcare for his daughter.

Now we have three elements: hope as an *attitude*, hope as *imagination*, and hope as *behaviors*. We may well imagine that Jack also experiences hope as a *feeling*, especially when his actions garner some success. At least part of Jack's hope is his *belief* that his life situation could improve. Adrienne Martin says hope sometimes expresses itself in forms of *attention* or perception; that is, Jack might see or interpret events in his life as leading toward desired object-states.

Some people in Jack's situation would despair. Jack could despair. But he doesn't have to. He can hope.

Jack's hope fits Bishop's description of a positive causal network. The various elements of Jack's hope reinforce each other. They cohere in a homeostatic property cluster, which can endure, in the face of many discouragements, for a lifetime.

Many people have observed that hope can sustain people in harsh circumstances. Bishop's network theory may help explain why this is. More precisely, his theory gives a framework for psychological research, and that research may explain how we may learn to hope.

In 1 Thessalonians, perhaps the first New Testament document written, Paul thanks God for his readers' "work produced by faith, labor prompted by love, and endurance inspired by hope" (Rom 5:4). This is a familiar idea, that hope helps us endure hard times. Later on, however, Paul wrote in the Letter to the Romans that Christians should "rejoice in sufferings, because suffering produces perseverance; perseverance, character; and character, hope" (1 Thess 1:3). The idea here seems to be that hard times lead to hope. The Bible reader might be led to object, which is it? Does hope sustain us in hard times, or do hard times help us develop hope?

Both. Practical experience teaches that a right response to hard times encourages hope and that hope helps us keep going in hard times. Bishop's network theory of positive psychology helps us conceptualize the matter. Hope is not only an attitude we adopt toward life; it is a syndrome of perceptions, feelings, beliefs, and behaviors that reinforce each other. Hope is, in Bishop's terms, a positive causal network.

Snyder's hope theory emphasizes part of this causal network; the part where cognitive changes drive affective changes. But hope is complicated, and the noncognitive elements (behaviors, feelings, motivations) can reinforce the cognitive parts.

Scioli and Biller: Motives for Hope

Adrienne Martin and Michael Bishop write as philosophers. Martin explicitly criticizes Snyder's theory as too simplistic, and Bishop's theory of positive psychology can be interpreted as making the same criticism. Psychologists Anthony Scioli and Henry Biller wrote *Hope in the Age of Anxiety* before the publication of Martin or Bishop's work.[20] They criticize Snyder's hope theory as being too strongly cognitive and mastery oriented (that is, directed at specific goals). Once again, hope emerges as something more complicated than Snyder's theory allows.

The core definition of hope says we desire certain object-states. Scioli and Biller's work presses us to ask *why*. Not all desires have the same motive. They say we can gain insight into hope if we ask why we want the things we hope for.

Scioli and Biller take cues from evolutionary psychology and empirical research to theorize that hope has three basic motives: mastery (achieving goals), attachment (connecting with other persons), and survival (extending life and finding purpose in the face of death). A defender of Snyder's hope theory could argue that mastery, attachment, and survival fit neatly into Snyder's teleological scheme; they name three kinds of goals. But Scioli and Biller ask us to look more carefully. In *mastery*, we try to

20. Scioli and Biller, *Hope in the Age of Anxiety*.

assert power over some aspect of the world. In *attachment*, we seek relationship with other persons. In *survival*, we try to defeat death, either directly by gaining an afterlife or indirectly by finding lasting significance for one's life. Since relationships with other persons depend at least partly on those persons, hopes for attachment differ in important ways from hopes for mastery (gaining skills, succeeding in projects, etc.). Religious ideas of a good afterlife often involve God, and other forms of lasting life significance may depend partly on judgments made by others, so survival hopes also should be distinguished from mastery goals.

Scioli and Biller say the basic desires for mastery, attachment, and survival have deep evolutionary roots. But the way they are experienced by individuals is shaped by culture, religion, and personal history. For example, in some cultures a person's ancestors are thought to be part of the community, so the individual seeks attachment not only to people still living but to prior generations. A different aspect: early in someone's life, the motive of attachment moves her to seek connections with parents and friends at school, but in old age many of her attachments are maintained by memory since her companions have died. Depending on a person's age and health, his survival motive may focus literally on living longer, or it may seek reassurance that his life had meaning.

The motives of attachment and survival obviously raise religious questions. Does God exist so that one can seek attachment to God? If there is an afterlife for human beings, what is it like? Can human solidarity and community stretch across generations to include those long dead? Scioli and Biller take a pluralist approach to the world's religions, treating them all as useful ways of maintaining hope.[21] What about atheists? Obviously, an atheist can hope for many things, but can she hope in the face of inevitable death? Scioli and Biller mention Bertrand Russell, who explicitly rejected religious ideas and honestly struggled with the passions that preoccupied him: love, knowledge, and pity for human beings who suffer.[22] Without endorsing this or that religious or nonreligious worldview, Scioli and Biller urge their readers to seek deep grounding for hope. Scioli and Biller write as therapists; in an "age of anxiety" they want their readers to hope. They recognize that hope forces us to ask religious questions, but they don't settle on one answer rather than others. They urge their readers to find something that will work for them. Before turning to questions of transcendence

21. Scioli and Biller, *Hope in the Age of Anxiety*, 76–92.
22. Scioli and Biller, *Hope in the Age of Anxiety*, 91.

and religion in chapter 6, I want to discuss some practical matters arising from the psychology of hope in chapter 5.

For now, a summary: *hope is a positive causal network of feelings, thoughts, actions, perceptions, and/or motivations aimed at a future object-state judged (implicitly or explicitly) to be good and possible (neither impossible nor certain).*

Put more simply: *hope is a syndrome of psychological elements aimed at an object-state judged to be good and possible.*

5

From Theory to Practice

S ummary from chapter 4: *hope is a positive causal network of feelings, thoughts, actions, perceptions, and/or motivations aimed at a future object-state judged (implicitly or explicitly) to be good and possible (neither impossible nor certain).*

Such a definition of hope provokes practical questions, "practical" in Socrates or Aristotle's sense, addressing the way we should live: How does one hope? What should one hope for?

The answers to these questions will be complicated, for three reasons. First, the *elements* of a hope syndrome are varied, including beliefs, perceptions, feelings, actions, and motivations. Second, the *object-states* we desire also vary, and the differences between them are practically (morally) significant. Third, particular aspects of different object-states emphasize different elements in a syndrome of hope.

Finding Fragments: Elements of a Hope Syndrome

Suppose a new client makes an appointment with one of Charles Snyder's hope therapy psychologists. Filling out initial paperwork, the patient, who could be a man or woman, complains of lethargy, anxiety, and depression. The doctor directs the client to complete one or more of the hope scales invented by Snyder's research team. Unsurprisingly, the client scores low on the hope scales. Almost certainly, the doctor concludes, her new client would feel better and make greater progress toward the client's life goals if he or she had more hope.

We can imagine a bit of sarcasm on the part of the client. "Well, sure. I *would* feel better if I had more hope, but I don't. I'm depressed. *How* can I hope?"

Guided by Snyder's theory, hope therapists don't directly address their clients' feelings. Instead, they inquire about the clients' goals. What projects would they like to complete? Which relationships would they like to improve? And so on. With help, most people can readily create a list of personally compelling goals.

What prevents the client from reaching his or her goals? Clients can usually identify at least some of the things blocking them from their goals, and skillful counselors can help them dig a little deeper. For example: "The job I want requires a certification of a particular kind, which I don't have. . . . Yes, the certification is available, but the nearest school is forty miles away."

The hope therapist may explicitly explain hope theory. "In order to be hopeful, you need to believe that you can think up pathways around your blocks *and* you need to believe that you have the motivation to use those pathways. It seems you have already thought of at least one pathway around the block if you had a way to attend the school."

Sometimes, when exploring a client's goals, the client will express doubt about his or her motivation. "I'm depressed. I don't know if I have motivation." The therapist can point out that the client has already demonstrated some level of motivation (and pathways thinking), because the fact the client has sought out therapy shows motivation to move forward.

Baby steps. Hope therapists help clients to break down big goals into manageable stages. What at first seemed like a single enormous block to one's goal turns out to be a series of small blocks. One by one, the patient thinks of ways around the obstacles. With repeated success the client learns to think: "I can think of pathways to my goal and I am determined to use them."

Over time, the client's depression and anxiety lessens. He or she is learning to hope, and hope brings with it an improved emotional state. The patient *feels* hopeful.

Now, let's step back to reflect on our example. The story gives Snyder's answer to the practical question, "How does one hope?" According to hope theory, we learn to hope by focusing on *beliefs*, in particular the belief that we can imagine pathways to our goals and the belief that we are motivated to use those pathways.

Anthony Scioli and Henry Biller criticize Snyder's theory as being incomplete. Hope theory rests on the notion that beliefs can drive feelings, which is true. What Synder's theory fails to acknowledge is that other elements of hope can also play causal roles, a point emphasized in Michael Bishop's positive causal network theory. Let's consider another example.

In late autumn, a man goes hiking in a forest in eastern Oregon. He parks at the end of a paved road and walks deep into the woods on a Forest Service road. There is a single pair of tire tracks in the skiff of snow on the road; the man has chosen this route and day partly because he seeks the solitary quiet of the forest. The man does not consider himself religious, but his hike is a kind of spiritual quest, an opportunity to commune with the nonhuman environment. A few miles into the wilderness, he wonders at a sound; somewhere off to his right an animal is moving in the trees. A deer, perhaps? The man leaves the road, hiking down a steep slope to a creek bed. On the other side of the creek, he sees footprints—not a deer, but something smaller, maybe a fox.

The creek, which would run high in the spring, is a mere trickle in November. The hiker easily jumps over it, but his foot lands on an ice-covered rock. His boot slips, throwing all his weight onto an awkwardly bent leg; a bone snaps audibly. Instantly, pain and the shock of injury cloud the man's mind. After a few minutes, he tries straightening the leg and almost loses consciousness in a wave of pain. Though it is agony, he discovers he can crawl with his arms and one knee, dragging the injured leg.

Crawling through the creek, the man realizes the extremity of his situation. He cannot possibly walk. His car is miles away. He is dressed well enough for cold weather hiking, but now his clothes are wet from the creek. Sunset will come early, and the night will be much colder. If he had a way to start a fire, he could stay warm through the night, but as a nonsmoker, the man carries no matches or lighter and he has no idea how he might build a fire. It may take all his strength to drag himself from the creek to the Forest Service Road. The solitude he sought out at the beginning of his hike now threatens his life.

Vehicles do—rarely—drive Forest Service roads in Oregon in November. The hiker remembers the tire tracks in the snow. Someone had passed through in the morning; perhaps that someone would return in the afternoon. Maybe some family will come to the forest looking to poach an early Christmas tree. When night falls, his friends/family will notice his absence; they will start looking for him. It doesn't matter to the injured man what the reason would be, he just hopes a car will come. Very slowly and with much pain, the man crawls up toward the road. At every moment he listens intently for the sound of a vehicle.

Again, let's step back from the example. The object-state the injured hiker desires is clear; he wants to survive. His injury and situation in the forest constitute a formidable block to his goal. He *hopes* that someone will drive along the road and rescue him before nightfall, or at least before hypothermia kills him. The hiker is doing what he can to achieve his desired object-state; he is crawling up to the road so that a passing driver will notice him. But there is nothing he can do to bring about a crucial part of his desired object-state; from his point of view, the appearance of a car on the road is a matter of low, though not zero, probability. In this case and many other cases like it, crucial parts of our hopes are beyond our control. It seems that "pathways thinking" has limited purchase here.

On Adrienne Martin's analysis, the hiker need not—indeed, should not—deceive himself about the likelihood of a car coming. Judgments of probability need to be made according to ordinary standards of evidence. The hiker may rightly judge there is a 1-in-10,000 chance that a car will come. Still, the hiker's hope can be rational—he may *license* himself to hope—because the coming of the car is so important to him.

Notice a particular element in the injured hiker's hope. He listens intently for sound of a vehicle. Martin says that hope is a syndrome of various elements, and among those elements is *attention/perception*. When we hope, we attend to the world differently. Remember Martin's example of Bess, the cancer patient. Having taken the experimental drug, Bess may pay closer attention to the days when she feels less pain. Because of her hope, she interprets certain features of her experience as signaling progress.

In the case of the injured hiker, hope could make the difference between life and death. Having reached the road, suppose the man huddles inside his coat. He waits, listening, all night. In the end, of course, he might freeze to death. But, as Victor Frankl noted in his experience in prison camp, hope can help a man endure another day.[1] In the morning, rescue might come.

1. Something like Frankl's experience is common knowledge among physicians:

Michael Bishop's positive causal network theory matches well with Martin's syndrome analysis of hope. There are multiple elements ("PCN fragments") of a positive causal network; in this case, the syndrome/network of hope. Often, as with the hope therapy patient, a change of *belief* will drive feelings of hopefulness. In the case of the injured hiker, heightened *attention* to some feature of the world may draw out the strength to endure. Bishop explicitly says that positive causal networks are made up of multiple parts. If we want to develop a PCN, we need to look for causal fragments that can contribute to that PCN.

Applying PCN theory to hope, we try to find psychological elements—fragments of hope—appropriate to concrete cases. How does one hope? In different cases, different fragments will come to the fore. *Beliefs* and *attention* do not exhaust the list. *Imagination* may play a role, as when Andy Dufresne pictures himself having escaped prison and living in Mexico.[2] *Making plans* ("pathways thinking") and acting on them can be important. And *hopefulness*—that is, an optimistic feeling, which is what Michael Bishop seems to mean by "hope"—can affect one's beliefs and plans.

So: How does one hope? The precise answer will vary from case to case, but in every case one finds appropriate psychological elements that can contribute to a hope syndrome, a hopeful PCN.

Varieties of Hope

What should one hope for? Here is a list, which illustrates some of the ways hopes differ:

1. Suzanne hoped to win the lottery.

2. Stephanie hoped for comfortable weather on her wedding day.

3. Hitler hoped to start a war by invading Poland.

4. Kennedy hoped to prevent war by quarantining Cuba.

5. Galadriel hoped Frodo's quest would succeed.

6. Lisa hopes the world will avoid catastrophic global warming.

7. Phil hopes the Mariners will win the World Series.

hopeful patients generally do better than nonhopeful patients. Thus, doctors often emphasize the positive, telling cancer patients how proposed therapies or medicines might improve their conditions or extend their lives.

2. Darabont, *Shawshank Redemption*.

8. The farm boy hopes the princess will fall in love with him.

9. Don Juan hopes to seduce his neighbor's wife.

10. Marilyn hopes to be raised from the dead.

It is important to see that desired object-states vary *morally*. Some hopes are immoral; Don Juan desires an outcome he thinks is good, but which is objectively evil. Other hopes are morally permissible, but not deserving of much praise (Is it really wise to devote hours of attention to baseball?); we might think of them as weakly good. Other object-states are morally praiseworthy, such as the hope to prevent global warming and Kennedy's hope to prevent a war.[3]

Object-states differ in regard to the *number of people* involved. Suzanne's hope to win the lottery and the farm boy's hope to win the princess focus on one or very few people. Good weather for Stephanie's wedding would please the wedding guests, a middle-sized group. Frodo's quest, if Galadriel's hope were fulfilled, would save all the free folk of Middle-earth.

Object-states also vary by the *degree to which an agent can contribute* to them. Hitler's decision to invade Poland almost guaranteed that his hope for war would come to fruition. As head of state, he had power to accomplish his goal far beyond an ordinary citizen or common soldier. Suzanne's purchase of a lottery ticket was a necessary component of her hope (the lottery commission often reminds us that we can't win if we don't play), but beyond that, her hope depended on forces completely outside her control.

---

3. A hope critic, such as Simon Critchley, could point out that Kennedy hoped to prevent war by means of a naval blockade (though he called it a quarantine), and a blockade is an act of war. As it turned out, Kennedy's gamble succeeded, so we are tempted to praise his hope. But we should not, the critic might say. If in fact Kennedy was hoping for a very unlikely outcome, his hope was irrational. Instead, he should have acted on the basis of likely outcomes. Adrienne Martin's analysis of the rationality of hope would say that Kennedy's action, aiming at a very important outcome (avoiding nuclear catastrophe), could be rational even if the likelihood of success was small.

This case shows that what we think about the rationality of hope will influence what we think about the morality of hope. The hope critic can argue that hoping for very unlikely things is not only irrational but also immoral. What would we say of Kennedy's hope if the "quarantine" had led to war?

This criticism conflates the hoped-for object-state with the means chosen to achieve it. Hope for a certain object-state is morally praiseworthy if the object-state is good. The means chosen to achieve a good object-state is a different question. Kennedy probably would have said that all his options were dangerous, and his chosen gamble was the most likely to avert war. Critchley and other hope critics might approve that line of thinking. There is nothing irrational about choosing the best of bad options.

Galadriel gave Frodo her encouragement and a gift of a magic crystal, but the outcome of her hope rested mostly on Frodo and his companions. Marilyn's hope for resurrection depends on God: that he exists and wills to resurrect people. Depending on the details of Marilyn's theology, she may believe that her resurrection also depends on her faith or her obedience or performing some religious ritual, but the possibility of resurrection comes from God, not Marilyn. And it seems that a baseball fan's hope has no bearing whatever on whether his favorite team wins.

Great Hopes and Individual Action

The environmental ethicists in *Ecology, Ethics, and Hope* worry about object-states to which a single person can contribute little. If we analyze hope on Snyder's terms, how does Lisa hope to avert climate change? The "pathway" to prevent climate catastrophe requires concerted action by governments, industries, and whole populations. What can one individual do? The environmental ethicists come close to despair because their hope depends on many other people choosing to cooperate with their vision. Millions of individuals must choose to do difficult things (at the least, things they are not now doing), and they must persist in doing those things for a long time. To that end, it would help if all those people had a lively hope that climate change disaster can be averted. But if they were well informed (i.e., if they believed the truth about anthropogenic climate change), each one of those millions would know the hoped-for object-state is almost entirely outside his or her power to achieve.

Let us say that a "great hope" aims at a *morally praiseworthy object-state that benefits very many people*. This is a vague definition, but examples will help. My hopes for my favorite baseball team would not qualify because those hopes, while not positively pernicious, do not aim at a sufficiently good object-state. Stephanie's hope for comfortable weather for her wedding aims at a genuine benefit, but only for a middle-sized group of people, not enough to make it a great hope. Marilyn's resurrection hope, if it focuses only on her own future, is not a great hope. If Marilyn's hope looks for the general resurrection of all people, it is a great hope (assuming that resurrection is a benefit; according to some theological views the great majority of human beings past and present will suffer eternal punishment after the resurrection; if that were true at least some people might prefer permanent nonexistence). Kennedy's hope to prevent nuclear war was a great hope. Lisa's hope to avert climate change is a great hope.

Perhaps all great hopes, because they aim for an object-state that benefits very many people, are like a Christian's hope for a general resurrection or an environmentalist's hope to avert climate change. A single person can do very little to achieve the desired end. This underlines what I see as a defect in Snyder's hope theory, because the "pathway" to the hoped-for goal is almost completely beyond the hoper's power. It seems obvious (to me, anyway) that some praiseworthy and important hopes are not well analyzed in terms of pathways + motivation.

Someone might point to a counterexample: Kennedy's hope during the missile crisis was both a great hope and something he could achieve. At the least, Kennedy was prominent among a small number of men in Washington and Moscow in October 1962 whose combined decisions would determine whether his hope was achieved. In his case, then, perhaps a great hope could fit Snyder's formula. But the proposed counterexample is imperfect. Even in that case, Kennedy and his advisors were deeply aware that the outcome of the missile crisis depended as much on the Soviet response as it did on their choices.

Hoping and Waiting

> Those that wait upon the LORD will renew their strength. They will fly on wings like eagles. They will run and not get tired. They will walk and not faint. (Isa 40:31)

A Hebrew Bible scholar, Howard Macy, tells me that the word translated as "wait" in this verse could just as well be rendered as "hope." A different translation reads: "those who hope in the LORD." I think there is something subtle and important here, relevant to our discussion of great hopes.

Hope is a *syndrome*; it typically combines thoughts, perceptions, feelings, motivations, imaginings, and actions. We think about the good thing we desire, we imagine what it would be like, we are motivated to act in certain ways, we perceive or interpret events in the world in the light of our hope, and we are encouraged or strengthened to carry on. But the various signs and symptoms of a syndrome are not necessary conditions; they appear differently in different cases.

Consider Marty McFly in the movie *Back to the Future*. By accident, Marty has taken a time machine (cleverly disguised as a DeLorean, a futuristic-looking car manufactured only in the early 1980s) to 1955. After a number of adventures in 1955, Marty wants to return to 1985. He and Doc Brown devise a plan to send Marty back to the future, a plan that requires them to achieve split-second synchronization between a lightning bolt and the position of the accelerating DeLorean. The wackiness of the story doesn't change the fact that Marty *hopes*. On the basis of his hope, Marty and Doc Brown take *actions* that put both their lives in jeopardy. This lighthearted fantasy connects hope very closely with action.

If we reflect only on cases like Marty's we might conclude that real hope always motivates action. We might say, "If someone doesn't act on his hope, it isn't genuine hope." We would be wrong.

Consider a more famous character, from a classic story: Penelope in *The Odyssey*. For twenty years, Penelope *waits and hopes* for Odysseus to return from the Trojan War. Marty McFly in *Back to the Future*, and Andy Dufresne in *The Shawshank Redemption*, took definite actions that aimed at bringing about the thing they hoped for. Marty drove the time machine toward the electrical connection at just the right speed and just the right time. Andy spent years digging his escape tunnel. But Penelope can do nothing to bring Odysseus home. Her hope is displayed in a kind of *waiting*.

Someone might note that Penelope's waiting and hoping was hardly passive. Penelope hoped that her husband would return and that their lives together would return to normal. She *did* lots of things appropriate to her hope. Most importantly, she did *not* marry one of the suitors; she could only marry if she abandoned her hope for Odysseus's return. And it was not merely a case of saying no; Penelope resorted to various stratagems to put off the suitors. For example, each night she unraveled the weaving she performed during the day. So: while Penelope's actions were not aimed directly at bringing about the thing she wanted, it is not true that she "merely" waited.

Let's consider, then, another character, Jeremiah, in the Bible. Now we move from fiction to history.

Jeremiah lived and prophesied through the final turbulent decades of Judah's independence, roughly 615–580 BC. In contrast to the official court prophets, Jeremiah predicted disaster for Judah. In the war between Judah and the Babylonian Empire, the Babylonians were going to win, he said. Judah's king was going to be captured. Jerusalem would be burned. Young men were going to die, and young virgins taken as war booty. No wonder some of his fellow Jews thought Jeremiah was a traitor. His prophecies were hardly helpful war propaganda.

Jeremiah's prophecies came true in excruciatingly painful stages. Babylonian king Nebuchadnezzar captured Judah's king Jehoiachin and most of Judah's nobles and exiled them to Babylon; he installed Jehoiachin's uncle, Zedekiah, as a puppet king in Jerusalem. But Zedekiah listened to nationalists and patriots, who said that God would help them defeat the pagan enemy, so he rebelled against Nebuchadnezzar. The Babylonian army invaded Judah again. The final disaster came in 586, when Nebuchadnezzar burned the temple, killed Zedekiah's sons (and put out Zedekiah's eyes, so the last thing he ever saw was the death of his sons), and exiled even more Jews to Babylon. Nebuchadnezzar installed a Jewish governor, Gedaliah. But before long, the patriots assassinated Gedaliah, so yet again the Babylonian army invaded to punish Judah. The patriots then fled to Egypt, taking with them a prisoner—Jeremiah.

Throughout all this suffering, Jeremiah consistently preached disaster and defeat. Judah's God was not going to fight for Judah, he said. God was fighting for the enemy, bringing judgment on Judah for a variety of sins. If the Jews had any sense, Jeremiah said, they should surrender to the Babylonians to preserve their lives. More importantly, they should repent of their sins and obey God's covenant.

As I say, it's easy to understand why many of Jeremiah's contemporaries thought he was simply a traitor. In reality, though, he anguished over the suffering of his people. (According to tradition, Jeremiah wrote the hauntingly beautiful Lamentations.) And at the nadir of his dark prophecy, he announced a "new covenant": "The time is coming, declares the LORD, when I will make a new covenant with the house of Israel and the house of Judah. It will not be like the covenant I made with their forefathers" (Jer 31:31).

Christian authors in the New Testament claim that the new covenant has come true in Jesus. Jewish interpreters, as you would expect, have a different reading of Jeremiah's prophecy. We don't have to settle that debate in order to see that Jeremiah models an important aspect of hope.

Picture Jeremiah in your mind's eye. See him counseling Zedekiah to reject the advice of the patriots and submit to Nebuchadnezzar—and then imagine his anguish when Zedekiah's foolishness brings siege and defeat. Imagine Jeremiah taken captive to Egypt by "patriots" who rejected his advice again. For Jeremiah personally and for the country he loved, everything had turned to ashes and gravel. In the end, he died a prisoner in Egypt, where he never wanted to go.

And still he hoped. Jeremiah could *do* nothing to bring about a good future for himself or his country. At one point in the story, God told Jeremiah to go buy property in his hometown of Anathoth. How strange! Jeremiah was no farmer, and he had no children, so no one would inherit his property. Jeremiah bought the parcel as a symbolic gesture; *someday* Jews would again buy land and farm in Judah. But that was the extent of it. Jeremiah's purchase was purely symbolic.

Still, he hoped. Jeremiah believed that God would bring about a good future for Judah, a good future so far from anything he or his contemporaries knew that it would require a "new covenant." Jeremiah hoped in a transcendent power, in *a good future that he could not well describe*. I will discuss the idea of "radical" hope in the next chapter. I will return to the notion of actions in accord with hope (such as Penelope's weaving/unweaving and Jeremiah's land purchase) in chapters 7 and 8.

How does one hope in a case like Jeremiah's? Hoping, sometimes, is a kind of waiting. Sometimes we can't do anything to accomplish our hope, but we hope anyway.

Hopes and Wishes

For some of my readers, mention of the "farm boy" and his hope to win the princess brings to mind a contemporary fairy tale, *The Princess Bride*. Others, fewer in number, will have thought of another farm boy, the "swain," described by Søren Kierkegaard in *Fear and Trembling*.[4] Kierkegaard imagines a peasant laborer, the "swain," who falls in love with a princess. The swain hopes the princess will notice him and return his love. He imagines marrying the princess and enjoying life together. The swain's hope is fabulously unrealistic, as Kierkegaard probably intended.[5]

4. Kierkegaard, *Fear and Trembling*.

5. Interpreters often disagree about what Kierkegaard meant. He created many pseudonyms and put some of his most famous ideas into their mouths. His pseudonymous voices don't always agree. Sometimes he will refer—apparently in his own voice—to fictional characters introduced by his pseudonyms. The "swain" is introduced by "Johannes Climacus" in *Fear and Trembling*; Kierkegaard quotes "Johannes," approvingly, in *Upbuilding Discourses in Various Spirits*. See Bernier's discussion of these matters in *Task of Hope*, 81–142.

Since I am not a Kierkegaard scholar, I say only that Kierkegaard probably intended

It's easy to imagine a modern philosopher's advice to the swain: "Don't fool yourself! Quit living fantasies! You are courting despair."

Interestingly, neither Kierkegaard nor his pseudonyms condemn the swain's hope. As told in *Fear and Trembling*, the swain eventually comes to see that the princess will never notice him. As long as it was possible, his desire for the princess was a hope; when he realizes she will never be his, it becomes a wish. We can wish for impossible things, as when a man wishes his deceased wife were still alive, but we can only hope for possible things.

Ordinary prudence would tell the swain to "get over it." Life often does not go the way we desire. Our hopes are reduced to wishes, and if we cling to those wishes, we invite depression. But Kierkegaard pushes the story in a different direction. In telling the swain's story, Johannes Climacus (Kierkegaard's pseudonym) imagines the swain building his whole life around his hope. The swain did not marry any of the peasant girls he might have, because he hoped to win the princess. The swain subordinated all his other hopes to this one hope. It is a *central hope*. His whole existence is tied into this hope.

Human beings hope for a great many things; in one sense, *too many* things. Some of our hopes conflict with other hopes; the time and effort it takes to pursue one object-state precludes pursing some other object-state. But human beings are cognitively limited (sometimes plainly foolish), and without even noticing our self-contradictions, we hope for contradictory things. The swain did not suffer from such irrationality. Because he subordinated his other hopes to the central hope, his life had a kind of order.

When the swain realizes that his hope is dashed, he feels terrible pain. There is no longer any possibility in this world for his hope to be realized. And yet, because it was central to his life, the swain cannot renounce it without renouncing the meaning of his life. He cannot hold it as a hope, but Kierkegaard says he can cling to it as a wish. As long as he keeps wishing for something impossible, the swain will continue to suffer.

But Kierkegaard does not say—as many philosophers surely would—that the swain should abandon his wish. The swain needs the wish, along with the pain it brings, because it is central to his life. Without this wish, he would no longer have *his* life. Kierkegaard thinks an *authentic* life should be chosen over a less painful life.

---

this or that. I am indebted to Mark Bernier, *Task of Hope*, for Kierkegaard's distinction between "wish" and "hope" and the notion of a central task.

As long as he clings to it, the swain's wish for the princess will remind him of the limitations of life in this world. In Kierkegaard's terms, the swain's *temporal* hope—because it is defeated, turned into a wish, and yet never abandoned—may drive the swain toward better hope, *eternal* hope.

Consider, once again, the hopes of Lisa and the environmental ethicists. They hope for a world that avoids catastrophic climate change, and they believe this can only be accomplished by cooperative actions taken by governments, corporations, and millions of individuals. The hoped-for object-state would benefit all humanity and the planetary ecosystem, so it is not surprising that for some individuals this hope has become a *central* hope. This great hope expresses itself in many parts of their lives: in the careers they pursue, in their friendships, in political activism, in consumer decisions, and so on. They hope in this way and order their lives in these ways, even though many of them would admit the likelihood of success is small. Kierkegaard, it seems, would approve, to this extent: by pouring themselves into a central hope, Lisa and the environmental ethicists give themselves vibrant, authentic lives. Kierkegaard would add that, if and when Lisa finds that her hope has been crushed—for Kierkegaard, all temporal hopes will eventually be lost—she can cling to her defeated desire as a wish, a wish that can push her toward transcendent hope.

Summary

Hope consists of a variety of elements. Differing components of the syndrome of hope will take leading roles in differing cases. We can learn to hope by finding fragments of hope appropriate to our particular case.

People hope for a variety of object-states: some morally praiseworthy and others blameworthy. Some object-states are open to an individual's "pathways thinking," but some hopes, especially "great" hopes, often depend on forces outside of a person's control. It is sometimes right to hope for object-states outside one's control.

When hopes are dashed, they can be retained as wishes. Often, as many philosophers would say, this is unwise. Clinging to impossible wishes only prolongs and increases suffering. However, Soren Kierkegaard suggested that we should not abandon our central hopes, because they are essential to authentic lives.

Prospect

In chapter 7, I will return to the notion of eternal hope, specifically Christian hope. Before that, in chapter 6, I will explore Jonathan Lear's idea of "radical" hope.

6

Hopes and Fears

I n chapter 5 I introduced the notion of "great" hopes, such as Lisa's hope to avert climate disaster, where an individual can do little to achieve her goal and she recognizes that achieving the goal depends on other forces (i.e., nature, other people, God, or pure chance). If some great hopes are morally praiseworthy, as I think they are, then in some cases we hope by a kind of waiting. For Jeremiah, hope consisted in waiting for God to act, while knowing that God's deliverance would come long after Jeremiah's death. In the remaining chapters I will dig deeper into great hopes and the waiting involved in them.

Radical Hope

Chief Plenty Coups of the Crow people lived his life in hope. At least, that is the thesis offered by Jonathan Lear in *Radical Hope*.[1] Plenty Coups hoped for a good future for the Crow people, a future in which they would keep their land and maintain their cultural identify as Crow. And he held to this hope in spite of his belief, grounded in visions he experienced as a boy, that the coming of white people to the plains would irrevocably change the Crow way of life.

Lear says this is "radical" hope. Radical hope looks forward to a good future even when the very concepts one uses to describe a good future have been robbed of their meaning. The Crow people had a rich traditional way of life centered on nomadism, buffalo hunting, and intermittent warfare against rival tribes. Their traditions included religious rites (such as Plenty Coups's vision quest when he was a boy), sacred dances, celebrations of

1. Lear, *Radical Hope*.

successful hunts and raids, and many other things. White domination *devastated* the Crow way of life; by this Lear means not just that the Crow lost their independence but that they lost what philosophers call "thick" concepts of the good life. For example, what does it mean to be brave? A philosopher might try to define courage in terms of necessary and sufficient conditions, and if successful he would give a "thin" description of the term. A Crow warrior would have described courage with reference to important and typical Crow practices: hunting, stealing horses from competing tribes, and planting a coup stick in battle. Each instance adds "thickness" to the concept of courage as lived out among the Crow. Given his belief that the coming of the whites would drastically change his people's lives, Plenty Coups had only the "thin" concept that the future would be good after the storm, without his people's traditional understanding of what a good life consisted in. The rich, detailed concept of the good life of the Crow people before the storm would change greatly, such that before the storm no one would be able to describe what a good life would be like afterward, but Plenty Coups still looked for a good future.

The indeterminacy of such a "thinned out" concept of the good life presents a problem. Following Adrienne Martin, I have emphasized the complexity of hope, that the hope syndrome may include beliefs, actions, feelings, perceptions, and so on. What does the hope syndrome amount to if the rich details of the concept are drained? Lear says that Plenty Coups believed and hoped that the future would be good after the storm, even though Plenty Coups did not know what that future would look like. It may seem as if such a hope is nothing more than confidence; that is, a certain feeling. But for Plenty Coups and the tribe's elders, hope consisted not just in confidence but in certain *beliefs*, i.e., that the Great Spirit existed and could communicate truth to young men.

Lear wants to make Plenty Coups available as an exemplar of wisdom for secular people. He recognizes that Plenty Coups's hope was grounded in religious beliefs. In one of Plenty Coups's visions, a great storm flattened all the trees of the forest, leaving great birds like eagles and hawks without homes. Plenty Coups and the Crow elders interpreted the boy's visions as messages from the Great Spirit, telling the Crow people to imitate the chickadee, a small bird with little power to prey on others. Like the chickadee, the Crow nation needed to listen and adapt.

Nevertheless, Lear denies that religious beliefs are necessary for radical hope. He says that the *goodness of the world* is greater than finite people can possibly know.[2] Even secular people may rationally believe this. After all, the world is very big and very old; human persons live in particular places for relatively short times. Therefore, Lear argues, even secular people can hold to hope even in times of cultural devastation.

Lear says nothing about which forms of cultural devastation might threaten his readers. What are the great anxieties of our culture? Disastrous climate change? Terrorists who obtain and use nuclear weapons? A failure of liberal political regimes such that, when faced with terrorism, liberal states collapse into authoritarianism? Technological horrors as depicted in science fiction dystopias? Each of Lear's readers is free to read Lear's interpretation of Plenty Coups in light of her own fears.

Radical hope is not an ostrich-like denial that bad things may come. Lear emphasizes the *realism* expressed in Plenty Coups's visions (and the interpretation the tribal elders placed on them). Native American tribes had no way to prevent the onslaught of European invaders. White trappers would be followed by white miners, white settlers, and white soldiers. The invaders would bring their own definitions of justice, by which they forced the natives off their land, killing as many as necessary to take possession. Crow leaders—to the degree they understood the situation in terms of realpolitik—knew that Plenty Coups's vision was true. *The storm is coming, and we cannot stop it.*

Our situation is different. We do not know that any of the "storms" we fear are unavoidable (though they may be probable—see below). It is possible that the effects of climate change will be mitigated, that terror groups will be defeated, that liberal government will meet twenty-first century challenges, and that we will gain the wisdom to rightly use new technologies. Nevertheless, we may say: *it is possible that a storm is coming*. Nevertheless, says Lear, radical hope enables one to look for a good future no matter how bad the storm.

Radical hope is not a Pollyanna belief that everything will turn out fine. *Cultural devastation* is possible. To whatever degree we experience devastation, the good future we hope for will be different than what we expect. Lear underscores the depth of the disaster experienced by the Crow (and other tribes as well, but his focus is on Plenty Coups's people). The Crow had to learn a revised set of moral concepts. Forced onto a reservation, courage is still a virtue—but what does it look like? Courage no longer means planting a coup stick in battle. Before, a daring raid to steal horses

2. Lear, *Radical Hope*, 121.

from a rival tribe marked a young man as brave, but now, under the legal system of the whites, stealing horses marked young men as criminals and fools. In such a changed world, what is courage? It may mean facing a new age resolutely, even when many traditional practices no longer make sense. As Lear understands him, Plenty Coups led his people to a new and deeper understanding of virtue and of the good life.

If one of our deep fears comes to pass, we will need radical hope. The concepts we use now to describe human flourishing may need to change. Jonathan Lear never makes this point explicit, but I think it is implied by his argument. Let's illustrate with contemporary examples.

Twenty-First-Century Fears

In 2017, the dictator of North Korea threatened that his country had intercontinental ballistic missiles to carry his nuclear weapons to targets all over the world, from Seoul to Seattle. Does North Korea actually have this capacity? Military and technical experts express some doubts, but it seems clear that North Korea aims to have such powers soon. Does Kim Jong-un merely intend to bully his neighbors? Would he actually use such weapons? We may *hope* Kim Jong-un would have sanity sufficient to restrain himself and never use nuclear weapons. We may hope that Jong-un means only to use the threat of nuclear weapons to persuade foreign powers not to undermine his rule. But what if Jong-un is as unstable as some news reports suggest? A foreign policy built only on the hope that Jong-un will restrain himself is precisely the sort of thing Simon Critchley opposes.

Adrienne Martin's analysis of hope, though critical of the orthodox philosophical analysis of hope, could well agree with Critchley. "Hope for the best, prepare for the worst," Martin says. The democracies should have a back-up plan in case the dictator acts irrationally. But can we imagine what that plan would be?

Suppose North Korea fired missiles and destroyed Seoul, Tokyo, and Seattle. The international response would be immediate and overwhelming, for no political leader could tolerate letting North Korea fire a second round of missiles. Let us suppose that retaliation, led by the United States, was carefully limited to strikes against North Korea. Let us further suppose (though it may strain credulity) that China endorsed retaliation against Kim Jong-un, so long as China was not attacked. Finally, let us suppose that somehow, either directly as a result of attacks on North

Korea or because of sabotage by Korean rebels, fifteen or twenty nuclear weapons were detonated in North Korea. What we are imagining is North Korea turned into an atomic wasteland, along with parts of South Korea, Japan, and North America.

This scenario is not the doomsday story that haunted the cold war, the annihilation of humanity. In the "Last Days of North Korea" story, most of the world's people would survive. But our future would be changed in unpredictable ways. Nuclear fallout would hit South Korea, China, and Japan first, but its effects would spread worldwide. Radiation poisoning would affect hundreds of millions of people. Just as important would be the social and political fallout—but we cannot predict what it would be. What would governments do to try to prevent a recurrence of the Korean decimation? What "lessons" would be learned by terrorist organizations? How would ordinary people around the globe conceive a good life in a post-catastrophe world?

Such questions help us begin to see what Jonathan Lear means by "radical" hope. To the degree that we cannot predict what the world would be like after a Korean war, we cannot say with confidence what a good life would be. We would suffer from "cultural devastation"—perhaps not to the degree the Crow people suffered but sufficient that moral disintegration would threaten whole populations. Like the Crow, we would find ourselves wondering what our important virtue words mean. If a tenth of the world's people suffer radiation poisoning, what would "prosperity" or "kindness" or "justice" mean?

The Korea example is not the only "storm" that might afflict our world. Let us consider a less apocalyptic, but equally troubling scenario brought about by the progress of medical science and technology.

Modern medical science has begun discovering the genetic and epigenetic grounds of many human conditions, from obesity to cancer to intelligence. In the twentieth century, medical science aimed to fight diseases by discovering antibiotics to kill bacteria, vaccines that could prevent infection, and developing a variety of prosthetics and artificial body parts to repair injuries. In general, the focus was on *external* threats to the body: chemicals, bombs, and germs. In the twenty-first century it seems the goal will be to improve the human body itself, changing its genes or epigenetic processes to defeat disease and extend life. The new medicine will focus on *internal* matters, the body's own genetic code and epigenetic processes.

Medical research is expensive. There is no intrinsic limit to the expansion of medical science; as soon as a cure for polio was discovered, researchers moved on to other diseases. Therefore, the practical limits on medical research are manpower and money: How many top-notch scientists can we recruit, and how many labs can we afford? In the twentieth century, Americans poured money into medical research through taxation (e.g., NIH grants), voluntary giving (e.g., Easter Seals, the American Cancer Society, etc.), and direct investment in private corporations. One result of twentieth-century medicine was the emergence of the pharmaceutical industry, with enormous concentrations of wealth for those who could patent new pills. In the twenty-first century, companies that commercialize genetic or epigenetic science will make even greater fortunes. In order to gain such returns on investment, such companies will invest and risk enormous amounts of capital.

Let's bring these two thoughts together. In the twenty-first century, medical science will be able to change the human body in more profound ways than ever before. At the same time, medical research will be more expensive than ever before. So here is the storm, a storm that comes incrementally, not as an explosion. The rich people of the world will get to buy the best medicine, and access to the best medicine will make them "better" people. When compared to the grandchildren of the poor, the grandchildren of the rich will be smarter, less susceptible to obesity, taller, handsomer, and much more likely to live a long life.

An objector might say this is true already. Life expectancy in rich countries already outstrips life expectancy in poor countries. But twenty-first-century medicine may *wildly* accentuate the difference. Suppose that by the end of this century there are a few million people on earth who are born with almost no likelihood of cancer, stroke, obesity, near-sightedness, deafness, or dementia. Suppose that these people, our grandchildren's grandchildren, grow up expecting to live 200 years. But suppose they also grow up knowing that most other people still die before sixty—and in their much shorter lifespan, many of them will suffer chronic conditions not experienced by the favored few, such as diabetes, hypertension, glaucoma, and so on. Crucially, suppose also there will be a well-founded expectation that the descendants of the very rich will be on average significantly *smarter* than the others.

How would such a "storm" change our concepts of a good life? Necessarily, any answer is speculative. It is possible (I do not say likely) that people would question basic assumptions of liberal democracy.

Democracy assumes that people are "equal"; because of this equality they have worth and political rights. Slogan words from the French and American revolutions of the eighteenth century are familiar to us: liberty, equality, fraternity, and inalienable rights. In the twentieth century, Adolf Hitler derided the notion of human equality. The process of evolution is essentially one of competition, he thought. The better human beings—the "Aryans"—would and should enslave or eliminate inferior people such as Slavs, Africans, gypsies, and especially Jews. Hitler advertised his racial ideas as scientific (evolution plus eugenics). Nazi eugenic theory was bad science, but for some people the appeal to science gave a patina of respectability to their doctrines. In the first two decades of the twentieth century, in Britain and the United States, similar thinking under the eugenics banner led to forced sterilization laws. Again, bad science was used to justify violation of liberal values.

Consider, then, that in the near future, in the twenty-first-century storm, a new version of the eugenics movement might actually square with facts: 1) medical science makes it possible to change/improve human beings, but 2) such medicine is extremely expensive, so 3) a small minority of the world's population will be improved, and this may produce 4) extreme differences of wealth, intelligence, and lifespan. In the face of such facts, what will be the basis of democratic equality?

We can, of course, hew to a time-honored distinction: human *worth* is distinct from and not derived from human *capabilities*. Though we have unequal abilities, we have equal worth, and every person must be treasured, including those with severe physical and mental limitations. On religious grounds, I endorse this doctrine. Every person is loved by God; every single person is infinitely valuable.

But notice that we do limit human privileges (and perhaps rights) in accord with capabilities. We do not let blind people drive. We do not let some mentally disadvantaged people vote. We declare some people incompetent to make basic decisions about their own welfare. We do these things though we know that someday we too may become incompetent—and we trust in the benevolence and wisdom of others who will have to care for us when we can no longer care for ourselves. Therefore: though we *believe* in equal human worth, we *practice* inequality of privilege, and we think this is a reasonable state of affairs. Equality is a slippery concept.

What happens then, in a foreseeable future, when the gap between the able (perhaps we should call them the "super-able"—Nietzsche would like that) and the ordinary widens, and widens spectacularly? How should those with wealth, health, power, and intelligence treat those lacking such advantages? Vice versa: How should the world's unimproved billions treat their betters?

A modern reader is shocked by that word. "Betters?" A medieval mindset spoke that way. Peasants needed to learn how to behave properly before their betters. Modern liberal democracy has left such thinking behind. Surely we will never go back!

That is my point, my fear. Given possible, perhaps even probable, developments in medical science, liberal democracy will face a storm in the twenty-first century. Anyone committed to liberalism, as I am, may find this a devastating prospect.

Transition to Transcendence

Worse things are possible than a limited Korea war or my "transhumanist" dystopia.[3] Nevertheless, Jonathan Lear says we may hope. We may hope for a good future, even if we are not sure what a "good future" might look like. We are finite creatures who live for a short time. Our species, on the other hand, consists of billions of individuals living now and indefinitely many generations still to come. Further, unless one adopts a radically anthropomorphic value system, the goodness of the world is not limited to human beings. One does not have to believe in God or any goodness that transcends the world to face an unknown future with hope. So says Lear.

Psychologists Anthony Scioli and Henry Biller would like to make a similar claim.[4] They point to examples of atheists like Bertrand Russell and Carl Sagan who expressed hope—not just particular hopes for short-term goods, but great hopes for the human race as a whole—based on their confidence in science and rational inquiry. For such thinkers, the patient acquisition of knowledge will lead to a better future. It's at least

---

3. "Transhumanism" is the study of the potential benefits and dangers of emerging technologies that could overcome fundamental human limitations, as well as the moral dilemmas produced by using such technologies.

4. Scioli and Biller, *Hope in the Age of Anxiety*, 90–92.

conceivable that such atheists could approve of "radical" hope, because we do not know what goods future science and technology based on that science may open up for us.

But Scioli and Biller theorize three fundamental drives manifest in our hoping, and *mastery* of the world is only one. When it comes to *attachment* atheism fares less well. Atheists desire and hope for human attachments as much as anyone, but Scioli and Biller point out that most of the world's religions (i.e., Australian aboriginal religion, North American native religion, Hinduism, Christianity, Islam, Buddhism, Judaism, and traditional African religion) all propose some form of transcendent attachment—to God, to the ancestral spirits, to the earth/cosmos, etc., in addition to human relationships. Very often, religious people report the sustaining power of hopes focused on such transcendent attachments. In the hard times—in prison camp, suffering cancer, having lost a war, or having lost a career—people of different faiths have testified they continued to hope for fellowship with Christ, closeness to the tribal totem, or some other transcendent attachment.

The third motive for hope, according to Scioli and Biller, is *survival*. The world's religions do not agree about the details of survival. Some believe in personal afterlife while others emphasize communal or cosmic afterlife. It seems that atheists must deny all such hopes.

Russell, Sagan, and other atheists could reply that people should abandon dreams of attachment to nonexistent things and hopes for anything but symbolic immortality; we should learn to be satisfied pursuing the only attachments that really count. Notice that this advice depends on the atheist's conclusion that there *is* no God, totem, or other object of transcendent attachment. Mere agnosticism would not justify Russell's advice, because if a transcendent relationship is even possible, one could hope for it. For their part, Scioli and Biller encourage their readers to pursue spiritual paths, even the spirituality of atheism if there is such a thing.

Radical Fear

Notice that Lear's argument for radical hope bases a conclusion about *morality* (radical hope is an option for us in the face of cultural devastation) on a *metaphysical* proposition (the goodness of the world is greater than finite people can experience). One doesn't have to believe in the Great Spirit to believe the world has wonderful possibilities. I applaud Lear's attempt to make radical hope available to secular people.

A word of caution, however: if one does not believe in the Great Spirit or any other doctrine of transcendence, Lear's reasoning can be turned upside down. Science teaches the universe is vaster and older than we used to think. Lear argues that human beings, living short lives on a single planet near the edge of a medium galaxy, experience a tiny fraction of the possibilities for goodness the universe contains. This seems true. But it is also possible that human experience touches an equally small fraction of the universe's possibilities for evil. Lear argues, convincingly, that radical hope is available to us. Unfortunately, his reasoning also opens the door to radical fear. Cosmological peasants that we are, we don't know which terrors there might be.

Consider an example. In the 1940s, Enrico Fermi proposed what has come to be known as Fermi's Paradox, when he asked the simple question: Where is everybody? Given what we know about the age of the universe (very old), the nature of our galaxy (billions of observable stars, so probably billions of planets), the possibility of evolution (low probability in any particular case but near certainty in millions of cases), and the facts of radiation (in particular, radio waves), we should be hearing radio programs from other planets. But we aren't. Where are all those radio signals? *Where is everybody?*

People have proposed lots of possible solutions to Fermi's Paradox. For instance, maybe intelligent life (any life capable of making powerful radio transmitters) is much rarer than we expect. Or maybe ours is the first species in the galaxy to reach such technological heights. (Most scientists would laugh at the hubris of this suggestion.) And so on: speculation abounds.

What about this answer? Perhaps in every case—thousands or millions of cases—in which a species evolved to master radio technology, that species also invented nuclear weapons, much as humanity did in the 1940s. (Fermi himself, when he asked his question, was working in New Mexico on the atomic bomb project.) Suppose that in every case—thousands of cases, at the minimum—the intelligent species totally destroyed itself. We might picture our galaxy as a collection of myriads of "suicide" planets, sprinkled among the far more numerous naturally uninhabitable planets.

I'm not trying to provide a probable, or even plausible, answer to the Fermi Paradox. We would naturally want some explanation why every intelligent species would succumb to self-annihilation. Perhaps there exists, unknown to us, some mysterious force of nature that propels intelligent life toward catastrophe. My point is just this: The horrors of the universe could transcend human experience in counterpoint to Lear's doctrine of the goodness of the world. The evil of the world may be greater than we can know. Lear is correct; there are grounds for radical hope. But by the same argument, there are also grounds for radical fear.

Is there any way to tip the balance from fear to hope? Yes—if we knew that the universe or God or karma or the Great Spirit *favored* goodness, we could keep a grip on radical hope in the face of any amount of evil that might be experienced in a human life, and we would not credit the possibilities of evil to the same extent.[5] In the next chapter I turn to a discussion of Christian hope.

Summary

It is not hard to imagine twenty-first-century threats that might undermine our thick concepts of a good future. Nevertheless, Jonathan Lear is right; it is possible to hope for a good future even in extreme cases, cases of *cultural devastation*. Unfortunately, the reasoning Lear uses can be turned on its head. The evils of the universe may be greater than we know. Is there any way to shift the balance from fear to hope?

5. Adams, *Finite and Infinite Goods*, 373–89, argues for belief in God on these lines. We cannot participate in morality as we know it, Adams argues, unless we believe that goodness wins out in the end over evil. And the only way to believe that is to believe in a good God.

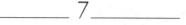

7

Transcendent Hopes

The moral arc of the universe is long, but it bends toward justice.
—Theodore Parker

M artin Luther King Jr. found this sentence in the sermons of a nineteenth-century Unitarian, Theodore Parker, and popularized it in
many of his speeches. Barack Obama liked it so much that he had the words
woven into a rug for the oval office during his presidency. Is it true? Does
the universe bend toward justice?

Chris Hayes, writing in 2018, said no.[1] Focusing on matters of racial
justice in the United States, Hayes argues that for every step forward toward equality between whites and blacks there have been important backward moves. Hayes counted as steps forward the elimination of outright
slavery after the Civil War, progress toward civil rights in the middle of
the twentieth century, and the election of an African American president.
Steps backward: the Jim Crow laws of the late nineteenth century, the *de-
facto* resegregation of public schools in the late twentieth century, and the
early twenty-first-century widening wealth gap between whites and blacks.
Hayes concluded there is no inherent moral arc of the universe: "Nothing
bends toward justice without us bending it."

Hayes wrote as a political commentator, not a philosopher. He paid
attention to just one moral issue, in just one country, and for just the last
200 years. Nevertheless, his criticism of Parker and King's sentence underscores the question I raised in chapter 6 about radical fear. Radical
hope, says Jonathan Lear, makes sense because the goodness of the world
is greater than what we can experience. In a parallel way, I suggest, radical
fear makes sense because the evil of the world may well be greater than

1. Hayes, "Idea That the Universe Bends."

what we can experience. Given that the universe is vast and long-lasting and that our experience of it is tiny and brief, it seems true that we know only a small fraction of the good or the evil the universe may hold. On what basis, then, might we say with King that the universe bends toward justice? Alternatively, on what basis might we agree with Hayes that the universe is indifferent to justice?

Given Adrienne Martin's analysis of hope, which I discussed in chapter 3, it might seem that we don't need to answer these questions in order to hope, even to hope for unlikely things. Remember that Martin identifies two judgments in "licensing" one's self to hope. First, there is the judgment that the desired object-state is possible, and if we agree with Lear that the goodness of the world is greater than we know, a good future is possible even amid cultural devastation. The second judgment concerns the importance of the desired object-state; a desired object-state may be objectively unlikely and yet still a proper object of hope if it holds enough importance to a person or group. If a person or society faced the kinds of cultural devastation discussed in chapter 6 (a Korean nuclear disaster, a transhumanist dystopia), it would remain objectively *possible* that a good future might occur. People of good will caught in such devastating worlds could "license" themselves to hope for a good future even if, in Lear's terms, they had lost their "thick" concepts of a good life. The hoped-for good future would be vague and hard to hold in one's mind, making for a weak "syndrome" of hope. Still, objective *possibility* is all one needs if the desired object-state is important enough.

Nevertheless, it seems that one's deepest beliefs matter when one contemplates great hopes. Great hopes depend for their fulfillment on persons or forces outside oneself. If one believes, as Hayes apparently does, that the universe is indifferent to morality, one will not hope for transcendent help. I take it that atheists like Carl Sagan or Bertrand Russell would agree: the universe may have more possibilities for goodness than we know, but we should not look for gods or angels to help us. We could hope that other people or that the progress of science will provide help. But if the universe is genuinely indifferent to our hopes, science may just as well discover new horrors rather than tools of salvation. We are on our own, so if our hopes look for *mastery* over problems (the first motive for hope, according to Scioli and Biller), we look to ourselves, to our science and technology.

Without a transcendent ground of hope, we should hope only for limited *attachment* to others, Scioli and Biller's second motive for hope.

Death—of the individual, of societies, and eventually of our species—will have the last word. Hope always aims for some possible good, and atheism rules out eternal attachments such as those dreamed of in religions. Our most meaningful attachments—to parents, teachers, spouses, and friends—last only until the other dies.

The atheist's response to *survival*, Scioli and Biller's third motive for hope, is similar. We may not like the fact that we live pathetically short lives in comparison to redwood trees or geologic ages, but it is better to get used to the truth than deny it. The few people who know and love us will remember us for a while after we are gone, but not very long. In a colloquial phrase: *get over it*. Hoping for impossible things is foolish. Russell, at least, did not shy away from these conclusions. It is better, he thought, to have clear-eyed hopes for real goods that may be achieved rather than waste time on impossibilities. To quote a famous essay from 1903:

> That Man is the product of causes which had no prevision of the end they were achieving; that his origin, his growth, his hopes and fears, his loves and his beliefs, are but the outcome of accidental collocations of atoms; that no fire, no heroism, no intensity of thought and feeling, can preserve an individual life beyond the grave; that all the labours of the ages, all the devotion, all the inspiration, all the noonday brightness of human genius, are destined to extinction in the vast death of the solar system, and that the whole temple of Man's achievement must inevitably be buried beneath the debris of a universe in ruins—all these things, if not quite beyond dispute, are yet so nearly certain, that no philosophy which rejects them can hope to stand. Only within the scaffolding of these truths, only on the firm foundation of unyielding despair, can the soul's habitation henceforth be safely built.[2]

We see, then, that when it comes to hope, metaphysical beliefs matter. Metaphysical naturalism rules out some hopes that theism encourages. A naturalist might agree with Lear that the goodness of the universe is greater than what we can experience, and that we may therefore hope for a good future in the face of cultural devastation. But that good future will not include friendship with God, angels, or any other imaginary beings. It will not include survival in any personal sense. And when it comes

---

2. Russell, *Free Man's Worship*, 5–6.

to help, as Hayes says, we must look to ourselves.[3] Nothing bends toward justice unless we bend it.

Martin Luther King Jr. was a Christian preacher, and Barack Obama drew his 2008 campaign theme, "the audacity of hope," from Jeremiah Wright, another Christian preacher.[4] As Christians, King and Wright did not believe in a universe indifferent to our hopes. Their metaphysical position offered them the possibility of transcendent hope. It is the goal of this chapter to explore such hope.

Vague Transcendence

It's helpful to recall that King found his famous phrase in the sermons of a nineteenth-century Unitarian minister. Today the Unitarian-Universalist denomination is the most theologically liberal of the mainline protestant churches. Compared to most Christian churches, the Unitarian-Universalists are significantly nonorthodox. In an ironic twist, they celebrate diversity of theological beliefs as the leading belief of their communion.[5] That is: the chief thing they believe is that no one's beliefs are false.

Now that sounds, and I think it is, incoherent. If one Unitarian's theological belief contradicts another Unitarian's belief, at least one of them has to be wrong. More charitably, we should probably take the Unitarian celebration of theological diversity as an unwillingness to condemn contrary beliefs on questions fraught with uncertainty. In other words: since we do not know for sure, we should not cry heresy. As a church, the Unitarian-Universalists are theologically vague.[6]

3. A possibility from science fiction: Perhaps someday humanity will make contact with intelligent aliens; is it possible that interstellar friends might help us achieve desired object-states? Allowing bare possibility to such a scenario, the tough-minded atheist could respond that wisdom requires we rely on ourselves, not alien saviors. And relying on transcendent help—from nonexistent God or gods or spirits—is worse than hoping for help from ET.

4. During the campaign of 2008, Obama resigned membership in Jeremiah Wright's church, in protest of some anti-Semitic remarks by Wright. Wright's role as inspiration for Obama's emphasis on hope remains.

5. See the church website at www.uua.org/beliefs/what-we-believe.

6. The "Seven Core Principles" of the church say nothing about God, any historical person, or spiritual practices. However, they do endorse goals of inclusion, democracy, and justice.

Nevertheless, this theological vagueness has enough substance to support Theodore Parker's faith: "the moral arc of the universe is long, but it bends toward justice." One does not need to believe that Jesus was divine (some Unitarians believe this, but most don't) or that he rose from the dead (again, Unitarians divide) to take him as a moral exemplar. In some sense, perhaps a very weak sense, Unitarian-Universalists take Jesus as a moral authority, and on that basis they can believe that ultimate reality (most Unitarians would say "God," but some would not) favors justice.

My point is this: transcendent belief, even the most vague and tentative, allows one to escape the view I have attributed to Chris Hayes, a view that is logically required by atheism, i.e., the universe is indifferent to good and evil and thus indifferent to our hopes.[7] When it comes to the object-states we hope for, it is atheism, often called "naturalism" among philosophers, that narrows the field of the possible. An agnostic might share Unitarian-style vague hopes, but the consistent atheist rules them out.

I do not say that atheists cannot hope, but they cannot consistently hope for transcendent help. In the modern era (roughly 1650–1950), many people believed in "progress" and on the basis of confidence in progress, they held great hopes. Notice that belief in science and scientific progress is not the same thing as belief in "progress" as modern people experienced it. In the eighteenth and nineteenth centuries, many Western thinkers believed that prosperity and education would produce not only new knowledge and technological know-how, but better people: wiser, kinder, and more just. But the twentieth century gave rise to a worry: *We are not getting morally better, and without moral progress, technological progress may be a bad idea.* We're not getting wiser or kinder, yet our technology gives us greater power to destroy. A characteristic mark of the postmodern age is its disbelief in progress. Individual atheists may still base great hopes on progress, but they ought to ask whether there is much evidence that progress is real.

---

7. The transcendent feature(s) of the universe need to have aspects of agency. It is possible to believe in transcendent goodness, e.g., Platonic forms, that are causally inert. In order to believe that the universe moves toward justice, one must believe that the transcendent thing/being actually acts on or in the universe. Thanks to colleague Ross McCullough on this point.

Christian Hope?

What counts as "Christian" hope? Most Unitarian-Universalists consider themselves Christians in some sense (some of them would like to shed the label), though their theology diverges significantly from orthodoxy. Besides the Unitarian-Universalists, there are thousands of different sects within the world Christian movement, and it is likely that their differences of belief imply differences in their hopes. How is it possible to speak of "Christian" hope? Are we to look for a common core among all of these groups? Where would we find those hopes expressed? In creeds or official statements by churches? In songs, hymns, and sermons? In surveys of ordinary believers? Imagine an empirical "super-study" that somehow accessed all these sources with the best scholarly techniques. We can imagine the researchers reading and comparing every church's statements of faith. They would collect millions of individual responses to belief inventories from members in every kind of church. They would watch and analyze thousands of hours of preaching, liturgy, and singing from around the world. If the goal were to identify a common core, the study would probably yield no conclusion, because the beliefs and hopes of practicing Christians vary so greatly. No study of the present hopes of actual Christians could define Christian hope.

We can, though, ask historical questions. N. T. Wright, in *Surprised by Hope*, argues that there is plenty of evidence to establish what the first Christians believed about hope—and why that hope was crucial to the birth of Christianity in the first century.[8] Whether Christian beliefs as recorded in the New Testament and early creeds should be authoritative for Christians living 2,000 years later is a matter for every church community to decide. Some, like the Unitarian-Universalists, could frankly regard past Christian beliefs as advisory only. Other Christian bodies might find themselves in a more difficult position. Officially, these churches affirm the doctrinal authority of Scripture and creeds, yet in their sermons, songs, and behaviors they distance themselves from early Christian beliefs. Wright alleges, with plenty of anecdotal evidence to back up his claim, that many practicing Christians today simply do not know what Christian hope was—nor, by implication, what it should be.[9]

What happens when a person dies? To understand Christian hope, Wright says, we first need to understand the thought background of the

---

8. Wright, *Surprised by Hope*.
9. Wright, *Surprised by Hope*, 13–27.

early Christians. What did the ancient world believe about death? We need not concern ourselves with beliefs in sub-Saharan Africa, India, or China at the time. No doubt these cultures were already developing the distinctive attitudes toward death that we find later in African ancestor cults, Hinduism, and Buddhism. All of these beliefs influenced Western thinking about death later, but the Roman world of the first century was mostly ignorant of them.

In the Roman world, there were three main answers to the question about death, plus a fourth to which Wright gives little attention, possibly because so few people believed it. The dominant view of the afterlife came from ancient pagan religion. On this view, people go to the underworld after they die. The gods punish or reward people for their lives on earth (though some denied postmortem judgment). On paganism, it's possible that the spirits of the dead may visit earth as ghosts or in dreams, so the pagan religious view could absorb and endorse beliefs from the popular superstitions of many cultures.

The second important ancient answer came from Plato. On this view, death is the division of a person's soul from his or her body. In fact, for Platonists, the real person *is* the soul; the body is just a distracting shell, which we should be happy to escape. Further, if the gods judge us in the afterlife, on the Platonist view they will do so justly, not capriciously, as many of the stories in pagan religion would have it. The souls of the righteous will enjoy intimate knowledge of the Platonic "forms": truth, beauty, goodness, and so on. Over time, especially from the third century and after, Platonic ideas exerted strong influence on many Christians' beliefs, not just on writers like Origen or Boethius but on the thinking of millions of rank-and-file believers. For centuries Christians have read and interpreted the Bible through the lens of Platonic dualism (or in modern times, Cartesian dualism). But Wright agrees with recent biblical scholarship that this is a mistake. As written, the New Testament documents were dominated by Hebrew ideas, not Platonic concepts, and we should be careful not to read dualism into the texts.

The third main doctrine about death in the ancient world was found in Judaism. By the first century, the Jewish diaspora, which had begun several centuries earlier, had established communities all over the Roman Empire, especially in the east, as well as outside the empire in places like Persia. Most Jews, except for a subgroup called Sadducees, believed in resurrection.[10]

10. The Sadducees rejected resurrection because it was not explicitly taught in the

Wright says we need to get clear about the content of this idea. Jews could agree with their pagan neighbors that after death people went to Hades, except that Jews called the realm of the dead Sheol. They might also agree about ghosts or visits from the spirits of the dead, since there were stories of that kind in the Writings and Prophets. Wright emphasizes that a belief in an afterlife as a "spirit" or "soul" is *not* what the Jews meant by resurrection. Resurrection was something they believed would come *later*. Jews believed that their God (the only God, a morally perfect God, not the fickle gods of paganism) would someday intervene in human history to establish righteousness and justice. On that future day, "the day of the Lord," God would resurrect all righteous people from Sheol to live in glorious fellowship with God. Some Jews believed God would resurrect *all* people, including the unrighteous destined for punishment.

Notice three features of the resurrection doctrine. First, in contrast to Platonic dualism, resurrection looks forward to an embodied human future. The whole person, not just his "soul" or "spirit," would be raised to life. Second, as with the rest of Jewish theology, the resurrection doctrine belongs to a linear timeline. In Jewish theology, God created the world at a time, made covenant with Israel at another time, spoke through prophets at various times, and would at some future time make all his purposes for Israel come true. The hope for "the day of the Lord" was universal in first-century Judaism. Third, the day of the Lord would bring worldwide justice and righteousness. Of course, Jews differed about what that would look like; some assumed God would ordain a kind of world empire with Jerusalem as its capitol and the Jews as God's viceroys over the nations, while others (the prophet Isaiah, for example) envisioned all nations equally enjoying the peace and prosperity of the age to come.

A fourth belief about death in the first century, which Wright effectively ignores as background for Christianity, is found in Epicureanism. Famously, Epicurus taught that the good life is a life of pleasure, not riotous partying but "freedom from pain in the body and trouble in the mind." Fear of death is one of the greatest causes of anxiety, "trouble in the mind." Epicurus found a cure for fear of death in the materialism of Democritus, a philosopher who taught that ordinary objects, including living things, were made of tiny bits of matter so small they were un-cut-able

Torah, the five books attributed to Moses.

It should be said that in addition to the Sadducees, the Jewish philosopher Philo also rejected resurrection. Philo was a Platonist, and his commitment to dualism would not permit a physical resurrection.

(hence, "a-toms"). Since a human being is a physical body, a clump of atoms, death is nothing more or less than the falling-apart of that clump. Observe any dead person as time passes; the atoms dissolve into something else. Therefore, Epicurus concluded, we need not fear death. After a person dies, she ceases to be, so she cannot feel any pain or trouble in the mind. Not even the gods, if they exist, can harm a person after she ceases to be. When it comes to questions of fear, the ancient materialism of Epicurus is similar to modern naturalism/atheism. There is nothing to fear in death, the modern naturalist says, because after death you won't exist. Interestingly, when it comes to hope, modern naturalists/atheists are not as comfortable with Epicurus. Epicurus's ethic focused on the individual and his intimate circle; he had no vision of wider or long-lasting community. Epicurus explicitly advised against involvement in commerce or politics, because such activities exposed the individual to all sorts of factors outside the individual's control. If you let yourself care about the world, you will experience more "trouble in the mind."

In contrast to Epicurus, many modern atheists extend their circle of moral concern to include future generations and the whole world; they would like to hope for a good future for people they will never know. On this point, modern materialist hopes seem more like those of the first-century Jew who hoped for an enduring universal kingdom of righteousness. We may speculate that the Jewish hope for the "day of the Lord," mediated and modified through Christianity over 2,000 years, has deflected our modern atheists from consistent Epicurean conclusions.

Whether or not that is true, Wright ignores the Epicurean/materialist view of death in the Roman world. It was a distinctly minority view held mostly by philosophers. More importantly, it played almost no role in the thinking of the early Christians. (Paul does refer to Epicurean thinking in 1 Corinthians 15:32, but only as a foil. If Christ is not raised, he says, we might as well live as Epicurus advised.)[11]

What we need to understand, Wright says, is that the Christian view of death is the Jewish resurrection doctrine, modified in crucial ways.[12] It was *not* a mere belief in life after death, as in paganism. Nor was it a belief in an immortal soul that has no need for a body, as in Platonism. These

---

11. This survey of first-century beliefs is not complete. For instance, I haven't mentioned the Pythagorean belief in reincarnation (similar but not the same as Hindu reincarnation). The popular doctrines, and their contrast with Jewish belief, are what's important.

12. Wright, *Surprised by Hope*, 40–48.

beliefs were widely affirmed in the first century, and Christian resurrection stands out in contrast to them.

Many centuries later, Christians confused their doctrine with spiritualist "survival" (akin to paganism) and the immortality of the soul (from Platonism) as well as other ideas that are further distant from the first-century thought world. Wright insists that resurrection is not reincarnation, nor the Hindu hope to escape reincarnation, nor Buddhist nirvana, nor any of our contemporary re-presentations of these ideas.[13]

How did the Christians change the Jewish resurrection doctrine? Wright lists several modifications of the resurrection doctrine in the New Testament. The two most important undergird the others.

First, in Christianity resurrection was a nonnegotiable central doctrine. In Judaism, some believed in resurrection (Pharisees, Essenes, Zealots), but some didn't (Sadducees and Platonists like Philo). In contrast, every strand of the New Testament makes resurrection essential to Christianity. Wright points out that this is even more remarkable when we remember that the Christian movement very quickly included many gentiles who would have been familiar with pagan beliefs, not the Jewish concept of resurrection. By adopting Christianity, they came to own a particular hope, distinct from any they had heard before.

Second, in Christianity the Jewish idea of a future resurrection is split in two. The Jewish expectation was that God would raise everybody (at least all the righteous) at one time. On the Christian view, a crucial part of the "day of the Lord" has already happened, as if the future kingdom had reached back into our time to establish a foothold. The Christians believed that in Jesus' resurrection the general resurrection of the end time had begun. Jesus' resurrection was crucially different from "ordinary" miracles of life after death, such as visions of Elijah or Moses or the raising of Jesus's friend Lazarus. Lazarus was raised only to die again. Jesus rose to eternal life, the life of the new age.

The first two modifications lead immediately to others:[14]

- Jesus' resurrection proves he is Messiah. Many first-century Jews expected a messiah who would conquer, but not one who conquers by dying and rising. As a result, they did not closely associate the messiah and the resurrection. For Christians Jesus' resurrection brings a new

13. Wright, *Surprised by Hope*, 9–12.
14. Wright, *Surprised by Hope*, 40–48.

understanding of what the messiah does and how the kingdom comes. Christians believed persons could enter the kingdom of God by faith in Jesus and receive the promise of resurrection life.

• Jesus' resurrection shows us what the new life and the resurrection body will be like. Jewish belief was vague about the nature of resurrection bodies, but the New Testament says our bodies will be like his. It is emphatically a real body; in Wright's phrase, Jesus' resurrection body "used up"[15] the body that had been buried. For this reason, Wright says the empty tomb stories of the Gospels are essential to Christian belief. At the same time Jesus' body is a *transformed* body, able to appear and disappear and transcend spatial dimensions.

• Since Jesus' resurrection has begun the new age, his followers live as agents of the new age. Everything we do "in the Lord" has permanent value (1 Cor 15:58). Wright is particularly concerned to correct the widespread notion that Christian hope consists of escaping from this world, expressed in songs (e.g., "This world is not my home; I'm just a-passing through") and preaching (e.g., that God will "rapture" Christians away from earth so that they need not suffer). In later centuries many Christians adopted such ideas and read them into the New Testament, but Wright insists that "escape" was not part of first-century Christian hope.

• Since resurrection is the heart of Christian doctrine, "resurrection" takes on new metaphorical meanings. Christian baptism is a "dying and rising." Christian discipleship and moral effort is "new life in Christ." These metaphors do not displace the literal meaning of the doctrine—that Christians will rise to life in transformed bodies; rather they add to it.

In chapter 8, I will return to some of these themes, in particular the idea that resurrection is the way that God's power produces the kingdom, and that Christians are to be agents of the new age.

So What?

If we think about it, there must be many other versions of transcendent hope. I mentioned the vague transcendence that grounded Theodore Parker's hope

---

15. Wright, *Surprised by Hope*, 59.

that the universe bends toward justice, and I've spent a few pages outlining first-century Christian hope as explained by N. T. Wright. There are many other great hopes, all of which rely on some doctrine of transcendence, only a few of which I have mentioned so far: reincarnation, the Hindu hope of escaping reincarnation,[16] Buddhist nirvana, the day of the Lord (still the hope of some Jews), Muslim hope in the mercy and judgment of Allah, the nineteenth-century Hegelian hope that the world-spirit would express itself in higher and better forms as time passes, and many others. Sometimes traditional transcendent hopes get repackaged with new terminology, as when a new-age Gaia worshiper hopes to blend her being into the world-spirit, which seems to be a reworking of Buddhism.

Some great hopes expressly contradict others, so they can't all be true. And some great hopes are incoherent on their own terms. For example, Marxism confidently predicted the coming proletarian revolution, which would eventually usher in communism and release true human nature, our "species being." It's safe to say that in the twentieth century millions of people died in hope, believing the Marxist gospel. But Marxist doctrine is expressly atheist and materialist. There are no gods or powers to promise a good outcome to history. To be consistent, Marx should have made league with thinkers like Chris Hayes: nothing bends toward justice unless we bend it. Why didn't he? I think the answer lies in the times. Marx was a child of the nineteenth century; he absorbed the confidence of modernism. Marx claimed to have started with Hegelian dialectic and stripped it of its spiritual guise; he called his doctrine "dialectical materialism." But the confidence of Hegelianism is rooted precisely in the elements Marx rejected, its belief in spirit (*Geist*) and the gradual outworking of spirit in human history. Without the spiritual aspects, dialectical materialism amounted to a historicist interpretation of history. That is: history shows a dialectical pattern, and it will show that pattern in the future.[17]

The most charitable interpretation of Marx's theory is that it claims that there is a law of nature (a law of sociology, perhaps?) that requires that human history move in a dialectical pattern. It has moved that way in the past, and it must move that way in the future. Interpreted as a *scientific*

16. In popular culture, the bare notion of reincarnation, that someone could have another life by being born as a new person, is a kind of great hope. This idea is borrowed from, but should not be confused with, Hindu beliefs. In Hinduism, the final hope is to *escape* from the wheel of rebirth. Obviously, both reincarnation and escape from reincarnation depend on some transcendent power outside the person.

17. See Popper, *Open Society*, for a thorough critique of historicism.

claim, Marxism was simply false, and it was seen to be false when the important "proletarian" revolutions came in preindustrial countries, 1917 Russia and 1949 China. Marxism as a *hope* died when the masses ceased to believe in its promises.[18]

I don't have space here to critically examine all these transcendent hopes. Nor do I have the expertise necessary to treat all the varieties of religious hope in depth. Therefore, the conclusions I offer about transcendent hopes are both cautious and cautionary.

First, radical hope, hope that persists in the face of culturally devastating events, is available to all of us, on the strong grounds that we have not experienced all the good that is possible in the universe.

Second, great hopes (all of our radical hopes will be great hopes), hopes that depend on persons or forces outside ourselves, depend for their possibility on metaphysical beliefs. In particular, naturalism/atheism rules out many of the great hopes that in times past have energized human lives.

Third, if naturalism/atheism is true, we should regard ultimate reality as indifferent to our hopes. It may be that the universe houses terrors we have never imagined. For all we know, every species in our galaxy that has evolved to the point of using radio has also discovered means of self-annihilation (our race discovered both in the twentieth century); *and*, for all we know, there is a causal law that such species always destroy themselves. In that case, the Fermi Paradox would be solved.

Fourth, human cultures are home to many transcendent beliefs, and these beliefs ground many transcendent hopes. It is possible that radical hope could be supported by these beliefs. Such belief systems should be examined for consistency and plausibility. The example of Marxism shows that a system of belief can bestow profound hope on millions of people and yet collapse from internal contradictions.

Fifth, Christian hope, as it is presented in first-century documents, is often misunderstood today, both by practicing Christians and non-Christians. In the last chapter I will ask what difference it might make for Christians today to recover Christian hope.

18. I am, of course, aware that the Communist Party of China rules over a sixth of the human population. But the CCP is much better understood as a gerontocracy in a Confucian culture than as the vanguard of the proletariat. The label "Communist" does not imply belief in Marxism.

8

An Ethic of Hope

But in keeping with his promise we are looking forward to a new
heaven and a new earth, where righteousness dwells. So then,
dear friends, since you are looking forward to this, make every
effort to be found spotless, blameless and at peace with him.
—2 Pet 3:13–14

A number of philosophers and theologians have suggested that we
need to think in terms of an "ethic of hope"—Gabriel Marcel, Jürgen
Moltmann, N. T. Wright, Jonathan Lear, and others. There is a great deal of
diversity among these writers; they understand hope in differing ways and
though they all think hope is important to ethics, they do so in different
ways. In this final chapter I will focus first on the underlying idea, that there
is some way in which hope should influence or control our moral decision-
making. In the latter parts of the chapter, I turn attention to specifically
Christian hope, again asking how hope should influence decision-making
and exploring some particular hard questions.

Hope and Behavior

Much of ethical theory, especially in the modern period, concerns actions.
It is assumed that moral philosophy should answer these questions: (1) In
situation x, what is the right thing to do? (2) Why is that the right thing to
do? To answer these questions, the standard ethical theories of the modern period—utilitarianism, Kantianism, social contract theory—all claim
to appeal to rationality. The right thing to do is whatever a rational being
would do in that situation. Of course, each theory gives a different account
of how reason is supposed to guide our behavior.

Partly because debate between modern theories of ethics has been inconclusive, the last half-century has seen a revival of interest among moral philosophers in "virtue theory." Ancient philosophers like Plato and Aristotle often thought about ethics in terms of character traits—virtues like courage, generosity, and justice; vices like cowardice, selfishness, and injustice. Starting with Elizabeth Anscombe's 1958 essay, "Modern Moral Philosophy,"[1] some philosophers have thought we might get around sterile modern debates by going back to the language of virtue. As a Christian philosopher I welcome the return of virtue theory. It seems clear to me that much, though not all, of the New Testament's teaching about morality is couched in virtue language.

Hope is a virtue. According to the apostle Paul, it's an important one, though not quite the most important. First Corinthians 13:13 says, "these three remain: faith, hope, and love, and the greatest of these is love."

Now, the revival of virtue theory provokes many questions, one of them concerning its relationship to action theory. Which is more fundamental to the moral life, behavior or character? Can action theories, which offer to tell us how we should act and why, make appropriate space for consideration of virtues? Action theorists might suggest that virtues are merely psychological tendencies toward good behavior, or virtues may be nothing more than actions repeated enough to become habits.

Conversely, can virtues guide our actions? A thoroughgoing virtue theorist might say that the right thing to do in situation x just *is* whatever a person with a well-formed character would do in those circumstances.

It would be philosophically pleasing to have a general theory here, one that explained how questions of character are subordinate to questions of right behavior, or *vice versa*. Unfortunately, none of the arguments I've read for one side or the other have been convincing. I think both features of morality, right actions and right character, are *essential* to moral life. Whichever aspect of moral life is most basic, it will be incomplete without the other. Whichever way one looks at it—that right action is more important and virtues are really just tendencies to act appropriately, or that character is really basic and our actions merely display our inner being—one could still hold that there ought to be an appropriate "fit" between behavior and character. Those who call for an "ethic of hope" assume there can be such a fit. Since this book is a study of hope, the fit in this case would run from hope to action, from character to behavior.

1. Anscombe, "Modern Moral Philosophy."

The place to start is with the general *structure* of hope rather than the content of any particular religion or ideology. Here I review ideas explained in earlier chapters. Hope concerns something (1) future, that is (2) desired, and that is (3) possible, neither certain nor impossible. Any philosopher or theologian who writes about an "ethic of hope" must imply that in some way such things (future, desired, possible things) should influence or control moral decision-making.

As we saw in chapter 1, the natural *passion* of hope focuses on future desired possible things. But the objects of hope as a natural passion may be morally neutral (e.g., my hope that the Mariners win the pennant) or even morally blameworthy (e.g., Don Juan's hope to seduce his neighbor's wife). Therefore, if it is true that hope should influence or control our moral decision-making, it must be a kind of hope that is directed toward morally praiseworthy ends. So far, then: *hope* in any possible "ethic of hope" must concern something *future, desired, possible, and morally praiseworthy.*

Let us assume that the object-state for which we hope meets this requirement. The central question for any "ethic of hope" is, then, "How should things hoped for influence moral decision-making?" At first blush, the answer seems obvious: in general, acting in hope would mean deciding to act in some way to achieve the thing hoped for, or (minimally) to act in some way that does not prevent the thing hoped for. An ethic of hope means deciding to act in ways *congruent* with things hoped for. We can express congruency in a two-step "principle of hope." First: *If and to the degree possible, an agent should act to accomplish the thing hoped for.* Second: *An agent should not act in ways that prevent or hinder the thing hoped for.*

In some cases, hope may require certain decisions; hope may create a kind of obligation. Consider an example from earlier chapters. In *the Shawshank Redemption*, life-prisoner Andy Dufresne hopes to escape from Shawshank prison. Over many years of imprisonment he acts, in a variety of ways, to accomplish his goal. Suppose Andy had "hoped" for escape but had done nothing—made no plans, dug no tunnel, accumulated no evidence of the warden's crimes—to achieve his goal? I think we should say, in that case, that Andy didn't really hope for escape. When a person desires a good future but does nothing to achieve it, we may be tempted to say he doesn't hope but only wishes for it.

At this point someone should object. Is it always the case that we can *do* anything to achieve our hopes? Remember another example from an earlier chapter. The Hebrew prophet Jeremiah told his fellow countrymen that the victory of the foreign empire was actually God's will; they should not resist, instead they should surrender to the Babylonians. After Judah was conquered by Babylon, Jeremiah advised his fellow Jews to settle down in captivity and pray for the peace of the city where they were captives. He also prophesied that God would someday rescue the Jews from their captivity. Now this was a message of hope for the exiles. But unlike Andy Dufresne, they could not do anything to achieve their freedom; if they followed Jeremiah's advice, they would express their hope by *waiting*. Of course, it was a certain kind of waiting, a waiting that resisted assimilation into Babylonian culture and religion.

Consider a recent case. Imagine an ordinary person who hopes that the Syrian civil war will end soon and allow millions of Syrian refugees to resettle in their homeland. I say "ordinary person" to exclude political leaders who might have some practical role in brokering ceasefire in Syria. It seems that most of us who hope for peace in Syria can *do* little to accomplish it.

This is why the first step of the hope principle expresses itself: "if and to the degree possible." In many cases, when you can take action to move toward your desired end and you don't, you are not acting in accord with hope. I might daydream about winning the lottery, but if I never buy a lottery ticket I don't *hope*. A single person may not be able to do much to prevent catastrophic climate change, but if she lets the enormity of the problem stop her from doing anything, she exhibits *despair* rather than hope.

I am *not* claiming that actions in accord with hope are always the right thing to do, all things considered, even if the thing hoped for could be a legitimate part of a good life and even if the contemplated action is within the power of the moral agent. I am leaving open the possibility that virtues might contradict each other.[2] If virtues can conflict, it is possible that practical wisdom might decree that in some particular situation I ought to act in accord with justice, generosity, or kindness rather than act in accord with hope.

The second part of the principle says that we should not act to contradict or prevent our hoped-for object-states. Sometimes we hope for transcendent goods, futures that we can do nothing to accomplish. Nevertheless, we might act in ways that deny or undermine those ends. Our

---

2. The so-called "unity of the virtues" is a time-honored debating point among philosophers. Plato thought that a person who fully exhibited any virtue would have to have them all. Many others disagree.

actions would express the vices of despair or presumption. The exiled Jews to whom Jeremiah wrote could have adopted Babylonian culture and religion. They could do nothing to produce the deliverance Jeremiah promised, but by assimilating they could contradict or prevent it.

There are millions of Syrian refugees fleeing civil war. Such an enormous humanitarian crisis staggers our imagination. We don't know what to do. We are tempted to turn off the news, either literally or figuratively by turning our thoughts to other things. This ignoring of the situation is a kind of despair. Turning away is an action; by it we act in accord with the vice of despair rather than the virtue of hope. If we are to really hope, we must at least not act in ways that contradict our hope.

Backup Plans and Forced Choices

Recall the discussion of chapter 3. Simon Critchley, voice of many modern philosophers, warns that actions based on hope can and often do lead to disaster. Acting in hope, the Melian leaders refused the Athenian surrender terms, resulting in death for the Melian men and slavery for the women and children. The modern objector says hope is at best a minor virtue that ought to be subject to practical wisdom. Critchley's advice: Be realistic; don't get your hopes up.

In contrast to such advice, Adrienne Martin says we can "hope against hope." It is rational and right, Martin says, to hope for very improbable things—in some cases, anyway. When we hope for unlikely things, we can keep a "backup plan" ready to hand. Bess licenses herself to hope the experimental drug will cure her cancer, but she also prepares a will, just in case the drug doesn't work.

Sometimes, though, we are forced to choose between our hope and the backup plan. Andy Dufresne plans and prepares his escape for years, all the while finding ways to make life in prison less horrifying (e.g., improving the prison library). But when he executes his escape plan, he is totally committed; if his escape is foiled, he loses everything.

Speaking generically, any "ethic of hope" must face the challenge of realism and forced choices. Is it always right to act toward one's hope? Failing that, is it never right to act against one's hope?

Imagine five explorers in Antarctica early in the twentieth century. Many miles from their base, the ice beneath their sleds breaks, revealing a hidden crevasse. The fall into the crevasse kills one of the explorers and destroys one of their sleds, leaving four survivors with too little food and fuel for the return. On the desperate trek back to base, the men begin eating the sled dogs; unwittingly they give themselves Vitamin A poisoning by eating husky livers. All four hope to reach base safely. But one morning three of them wake in the tent to find a note: "There is not enough for four. I pray there is enough for three." Their companion chose to improve their odds by walking into the dark.

They hoped to save four. The backup plan aimed to save three. It seems that sometimes we must give up one or the other. Can it be right to choose against hope?

Utilitarians approve the explorer's decision to sacrifice his life to help his comrades. In a forced-choice situation, they say, it is right to do things that would otherwise be morally blameworthy. In forced-choice situations, utilitarians say, it can be right to act in ways that actually *prevent* the object-state one had hoped for.

Consider the example a bit more. Suppose the three survivors met a rescue party the next day. They had no expectation of a rescue, but it happened. Does this change our estimate of the dead explorer's decision? Should he have clung to hope (that all four would be saved)? Another scenario: the four explorers hold to their hope, none of them sacrificing his life for the others, and as a result they all die. Does this change or confirm our evaluation of the original story? How long should we cling to hope?

Whichever way we answer these questions, this much seems clear: *any* "ethic of hope" is vulnerable to forced-choice situations. One may have to choose between the hoped-for object-state and the backup plan. Once Andy Dufresne makes his break, his backup plans for improving life in prison disappear. When the Antarctic explorer sacrifices himself to save his comrades, he abandons the hope of saving all four.

The above-mentioned principle of hope is only an abstract structure. To say more about actions appropriate to hope, we would have to examine particular hopes. What is it that we actually hope for? In what follows I resume the discussion of chapter 7, following N. T. Wright's exposition of Christian hope. Once we have the content of Christian hope in view, we must ask whether and to what extent Martin's advice about "backup plans" is relevant. If Christian hope is to guide our decisions, can we hold backup plans? Is Christian hope somehow invulnerable to forced-choice situations?

The Content of Christian Hope

The resurrection of Jesus determines the content of Christian hope. This is true in more than one way. First-century Christians retained the Jewish expectation that God's rule would last forever. After the resurrection, all the righteous will enjoy fellowship with Jesus in the presence of God. The New Testament uses a variety of images and words to describe the eternal kingdom: heaven, a wedding feast, the New Jerusalem, a new heaven and earth. Let us say, at a minimum, that first-century Christian hope contains:

1. Resurrection. Christians' bodies will be like Jesus' resurrection body.

2. Eternal life. Each Christian will have endless, conscious friendship with God.

3. Cosmic Redemption. A new heaven and new earth will be freed from decay.

4. Communion of the Saints. All Christians together will enjoy blessed community.

First, Christians look forward to bodily resurrection. This is a central theme of 1 Corinthians 15. The new body Paul calls a "spiritual" body, contrasted with a "natural" body. Wright and other Bible scholars warn that this is not a dualism of nonphysical against physical. That would be the mistake of reading Plato into Paul. According to Paul, the spiritual body supplants the natural body as a wheat stalk supplants the seed that was planted. There is *connection* and *change* in the transition. The bodies that we are now will be changed. We can speculate about these changes by considering the stories of Jesus' resurrection body, which was able to do ordinary things like cook, eat, speak, and walk; and extraordinary things like appear, disappear, and ascend.

A comment on ascension: According to the New Testament story, Jesus rose into the sky. Christians do not believe this means he is floating around in the clouds. His literal physical ascent symbolized a metaphysical or metadimensional ascent. Jesus is now in a place that transcends our places/spaces.

But now a worry arises. If the ascension story is taken to mean that Jesus transcends our places/spaces, isn't there room for a Platonic reading of the New Testament after all? Maybe our souls are immortal and they simply "go to heaven" when we die. It's safe to say that many practicing Christians believe something like this. A typical song says, "When I die, Hallelujah, by and by, I'll fly away." For such Christians, hope means one's immortal soul will go to be with Jesus, wherever that is.

Against this, biblical scholars like Wright remind us that in 1 Corinthians 15 Paul insists on resurrection in a spiritual *body*. A spiritual body is still a body. According to the New Testament, *Jesus exists in bodily form right now*. Perhaps the souls of Christians go to heaven immediately after they die, but they would then long for resurrection and reunification with their bodies so they could be like Jesus.

Further, first-century Christian hope focused on the doctrine of *parousia*, Jesus's return to earth. Early Christians expected Jesus to return "soon," so soon, in fact, that some were greatly disturbed when believers died before the *parousia*. In 1 Thessalonians, Paul reassures them: "We believe that Jesus died and rose again and so we believe that God will bring with Jesus those who have fallen asleep in him. According to the Lord's own word, we tell you that we who are still alive, who are left till the coming of the Lord, will certainly not precede those who have fallen asleep" (1 Thess 4:14–15). The emphasis is on Jesus coming *here*, not believers going there.

Some Bible readers would quickly object, for in the following verses Paul says that when Jesus comes believers on earth will be caught up to "meet Jesus in the air. And so we will be with the Lord forever" (1 Thess 4:17). Some Christians interpret these words as meaning that Jesus takes his people *out* of the world. But Paul is leaning on an image familiar in the Roman world: when an emperor came to visit a provincial city, the citizens of that honored place would go out to meet him and accompany him in a procession into their city.[3] Paul's image has Christians meeting Jesus and joining him as he establishes his worldwide kingdom.

To reiterate: Christian hope looks for a bodily resurrection in which our bodies will be like Jesus' resurrection body. Of course, centuries have passed since Jesus' resurrection, and billions of Christians have died. The general resurrection has not yet happened. What is the current state of deceased believers? Not surprisingly, the New Testament says little about this question, since early Christians expected Jesus' return soon. There is a passage (Rev 6:9–10) that describes a scene in heaven and speaks of the "souls of those who had been slain because of the word of God," who plead with God to bring an end to their long wait. One might conclude,

3. See Wright's discussion of 1 Thessalonians 4 in *Surprised by Hope*, 131–33.

then, that the souls of dead believers are in heaven already. But at most this would be a temporary state for a soul waiting for a transformed body. As Wright says, we need to think of what happens *after* the afterlife.[4] In the New Testament, the goal is always resurrection.

Second, Christian hope looks for everlasting life. In the resurrection, we will share in Jesus' life, and he lives forever. Historically, there has been little controversy among Christians about this doctrine. True, Christian theologians and philosophers have debated different views of God's eternity, some saying that God exists *timelessly*, outside of time, and others arguing that God exists *everlastingly*, with no beginning or end of time. Whichever view is right, or if some other description of God's eternity is correct, first-century Christians hoped to share in the life of God, a life that would never end. At every point, New Testament hope looks forward to personal fellowship with God.

Third, Christian hope looks for cosmic redemption. We look for a new heaven and a new earth, where righteousness dwells. We look for a New Jerusalem "coming down out of heaven from God" (Rev 21:2).

Wright says that the New Testament doctrine of resurrection must be understood in the context of the doctrine of creation.[5] God created a *good* world, which is infected with *evil*. The two-sidedness of this doctrine avoids two errors: the Platonic idea that the physical world is inherently evil, which leads to a "hope" of escaping to the realm of the forms; and a pantheistic/ progressive idea that since the world is good, it will develop naturally into better and better stages all on its own. On the Jewish view, which the New Testament adopts, God acts to change the world from what it is into what it should be, at "the day of the Lord." Wright says the New Testament gives us an eschatological dualism (the present age and the age to come) rather than an ontological dualism (evil "earth" and good "heaven").[6]

Fourth, Christian hope looks for a blessed community. Jesus commanded his followers to love each other. Paul calls the church the body of Christ. It might seem obvious that Christians should never fight with each other over ethnicity, material goods, national boundaries, political allegiances, scientific theories, or even theological disagreements. Unfortunately, 2,000 years of church history is full of such fights. The church is

---

4. Wright, *Surprised by Hope*, 36.
5. Wright, *Surprised by Hope*, 94.
6. Wright, *Surprised by Hope*, 95.

not yet the blessed community; we still *hope* for a blessed community to come.

The Challenges of Christian Hope

How should Christian hope as just described—bodily resurrection, eternal life, cosmic redemption, and a blessed community—influence or control a Christian's moral decisions?

Recall the two-step "principle of hope" I mentioned above. (1) If and to the degree possible, an agent should act to accomplish the thing hoped for. (2) An agent should not act in ways that prevent or hinder the thing hoped for. For Christians, the principle could be expressed in a single sentence: *Christian life here and now should be congruent with the life of the age to come.* We might paraphrase Peter's words at the head of this chapter, "Since we are looking for a heaven and earth where righteousness dwells, we ought to live that way now."

If this principle were sound, Christian hope would be central to Christian ethics. No matter what moral issue confronted us, we would ask: What is the object-state we desire? What are we looking forward to in the New Jerusalem? How will we behave on the new earth under the new heaven? And so on. The presumption is that the standards of the age to come should govern our lives now.

Here's an application/illustration.

In the new age, Jesus' people from every language and ethnic group on earth will rejoice and praise God together. Therefore, the church today should seek to be congruent with the blessed community, and that implies at least two things. First, we should preach the good news of Jesus to everyone (worldwide evangelism). Second, we should actively work to welcome and empower marginalized groups so that all persons are equally valued (social justice).[7]

So far so good, right? *Christian life now should be congruent with the life of the age to come.*

The principle may be misleading, stated so simply. An example: the Sadducees, who denied the resurrection, confronted Jesus with a

7. I am happy to say that George Fox University President Robin Baker has made this reasoning explicit in public addresses. The reason the university strives to attract a diverse student body and hire and retain diverse faculty is that we serve the church, which itself is looking forward to the kingdom of God, which includes every ethnicity.

philosopher's tale (i.e., something that might have happened, a theoretical possibility) about a woman whose seven husbands died, one after another. Now, if they were all raised, the woman would be wife to seven men![8] Surely that would be wrong, the Sadducees thought, so something must be wrong with the idea of resurrection. Jesus replied that in the resurrection men would not marry and women would not be given in marriage (Matt 22:30). The Sadducees' argument rested on an assumption about what resurrection life would be like, i.e., that bodily resurrection implies sex and marriage. Jesus overturned the assumption, so their argument collapsed. Now, the principle of hope might fail to guide our lives for similar reasons. That is, we might wrongly think that resurrection life will have certain features, and then, applying the principle of hope, think that we ought to live now in accord with those features.

Therefore, we need caution. The principle of hope should guide our lives now just to the degree we are confident that God really intends the object-state of our hope. When Christians disagree about what God intends for the new age, they may legitimately disagree about how we should live now.

Further reflection on the Sadducees' error suggests another difficulty. The fact that there will be no marrying in the resurrection does not imply we should abandon marriage now. We expect there will be significant differences between human life now and life in the age to come, which means that reflection on the age to come may not clearly direct us in this age.

For example, people of this age commit murder, but we presume there will be no murders after the resurrection. (There will, of course, be murderers in the new age; redeemed sinners of every sort will be present.) As long as we live in this world, our moral duties include appropriate responses to murder. Since there will be no murder in the age to come, how do we judge which of our possible responses to murder is consistent with the life of the age to come? Obviously, we ought not to commit murder, and we ought to try to reduce or eliminate murders. A society without murder would to that extent be congruent with heaven. But this does not tell us *how* to reduce the incidence of murder in this age. A parallel example: in this age, nations wage wars; Jesus' reign in the age to come guarantees peace. To be

---

8. The Hebrew Bible gives us examples of polygamy—more precisely, polygyny—being practiced and apparently approved: Abraham, Jacob, David, Solomon, and others. But Jewish scripture and culture never approved of *polyandry*. The Sadducees' story was especially powerful, they thought, because it showed how belief in resurrection led to an outlandish result.

congruent with the age to come, all Christians would agree that they ought to be peacemakers in this age, but they do not agree *how*.

Therefore, more caution is required. We face moral issues in this life that will not recur in resurrection life. Christians might agree that life in the New Jerusalem will have a certain feature but disagree about the relevance or importance of that feature for our life now. The principle of hope requires that our lives here and now should be congruent with life in the age to come, but congruency may be a matter of degree; it will certainly be a matter of disagreement.

Resurrection as God's Way

The examples just mentioned—murder and war—raise the question, "How?"

The two-step principle of hope says that Christians ought to act in accord with their hope; at the minimum they ought not to contradict their hope. How should we do that when the present age, filled with murder and war, is so different from the age to come?

I suggest that the resurrection of Jesus determines not only the content of Christian hope, the object-state for which we hope; it should also direct our *methods* of hope, the ways we attempt to live congruently with hope. Christ's resurrection tells us not only what to hope for, but how to live into that hope. The basic idea is a familiar one in theology: God defeated his enemies through Jesus' cross and resurrection. *God wins through Jesus' death and resurrection.*

Soteriologically, all Christian theologians agree on this point; salvation comes to us through Jesus' death and resurrection. They agree that, because of Jesus' death and resurrection, we have forgiveness of sins and new life. As Paul wrote in Romans 6:3–4: "Don't you know that all of us who were baptized into Christ Jesus were baptized into his death? We were therefore buried with him through baptism into death in order that, just as Christ was raised from the dead through the glory of the Father, we too may live a new life."

However, many practicing Christians deny or greatly restrict the *ethical* implications of the resurrection. I argue for a radical conclusion, which makes the ethical implications of soteriology explicit: *Resurrection is God's way of fighting, of overcoming opposition.* This conclusion is so counter to worldly wisdom that we need to meditate on it at some length.

The apostle James contrasted worldly wisdom against the wisdom from heaven:

> If you harbor bitter envy and selfish ambition in your hearts, do not boast about it or deny the truth. Such "wisdom" does not come down from heaven but is earthly, unspiritual, of the devil. For where you have envy and selfish ambition, there you find disorder and every evil practice.
>
> But the wisdom that comes from heaven is first of all pure, then peace-loving, considerate, submissive, full of mercy and good fruit, impartial and sincere. Peacemakers who sow in peace raise a harvest of righteousness. (Jas 3:14–18)

How does the world hope? By what mechanisms do the people of this age attempt to achieve their desired object-states? Some examples: they hope to get a good job or career by means of education, work, or good luck; they hope to hold onto possessions by means of bank accounts, investments, and security guards; they hope to secure tranquil lives through police forces and well-organized states. We use the powers of politics and markets to give us *security*.

The worldly wise hope to achieve *justice* by force, very often by violence. Worldly wisdom teaches us to find our enemy and "kill" it. Sometimes the killing is literal: war, justified homicide (e.g., "stand your ground" laws), abortion, or capital punishment. More often, the "killing" is metaphorical, though it can lead to death: fraud, poverty wages, denial of educational opportunity, exclusion of aliens, and others. "Killing" can also be rhetorical: slander, gossip, libel, or the simple deaf ear that denies the existence of the other.

Worldly wisdom seldom admits that "justice" obtained in these ways is not real justice at all. We admit occasional flaws—some mistakes were made, boundaries were stretched, noncombatants became collateral damage, a few innocents were wrongly condemned, and so on. Nevertheless, worldly wisdom insists that justice requires force and violence.

The worldly wise seek *peace* in two ways. First, peace comes after we have defeated the enemy so thoroughly that he takes on our values. The former enemy becomes a loyal part of our empire, whether that empire is British, Russian, Chinese, or American. General McArthur becomes governor of postwar Japan.

Sometimes worldly wisdom recognizes that the enemy cannot be beaten violently without risking catastrophe. Then we turn to the second

way of "peace," the balance of power. We match eastern bloc against western bloc. We try to limit our hot wars to this or that corner of the world. We
keep negotiating and we promote economic ties between the enemies. We
hope that the fragile peace may grow stronger if we give it time.

In sum: the worldly wise pursue security, justice, and peace through
coercion, violence, and manipulation. Occasionally some voices call for genuine dialogue, empathic listening to the other (e.g., cultural exchanges), and
even generosity. But these are unreliable methods. At root, when empathy
and generosity fail (and we know they will often fail), we must pursue security, justice, and peace through power—and power comes through knowledge
and coercive force and the willingness to use them.

Here's my claim. I argue that resurrection hope stands firmly against
worldly wisdom. As James wrote, we need to attend to the wisdom from
heaven.

Jesus taught his followers to love God first of all. After that, they were
to love each other. Jesus displayed his doctrine of love in the way he lived.
He offered forgiveness and grace to sinners, he healed mentally diseased
people, he taught poor people and treated them with dignity, he spoke
against religious legalists who made life hard for poor folk, he directly opposed the religious establishment that had made backroom deals with an
oppressive government, and he preached that God's righteous kingdom
was coming. It is no surprise that Jesus made enemies among powerful
people, religiously powerful people and militarily powerful people. After
Jesus' public protest at the temple of God, where the religious elite used
temple procedures to make a killing off the poor, it is no surprise that his
enemies marked him for death.

Jesus was a religious idealist. He thought love and faith would overcome greed, lust, and violence. So, they killed him. End of story; that is, it is
the end of the story as told by the wisdom of the world.

Resurrection means that crucifixion is not the end of the story. In this
story, the nice guy did not finish last. He was worse than last; he was never in
the running. Except for resurrection. Resurrection changes everything.

Resurrection hope means that we look forward to the kingdom of God,
not based on violence or manipulation or coercion. Resurrection hope *does*
depend on power, but not the power of the gun or the executioner. Resurrection hope says that when Hitler hangs Bonhoeffer, Bonhoeffer wins.

Bonhoeffer does not win by karma or by the pen being mightier than
the sword. Bonhoeffer wins because he is a soldier of the cross. He follows

Jesus and trusts Jesus. Bonhoeffer wins because Jesus' resurrection leads to Bonhoeffer's resurrection.

Ah! But . . .

The point of my meditation on worldly wisdom is supposed to be that Christians should act in accord with the wisdom of heaven. Since we hope for a kingdom of righteousness, peace, and joy, we ought to live congruently with that kingdom now. Since we are disciples of Jesus, we must be willing to die, but not kill. Christian hope should lead Christians to be pacifists.

Now, let's consider Bonhoeffer more carefully. At one time in his life, he espoused pacifism, yet when he could find no other way to effectively oppose Hitler, Bonhoeffer joined a plot to assassinate him. Bonhoeffer judged that he had to choose between "clean hands" and an attempt (even a long-shot attempt) to stop evil on a national/international scale.

One could argue that Bonhoeffer faced a forced choice. He believed the gospel calls Christians to be peacemakers. He believed the kingdom of God would be a kingdom of righteousness, peace and joy. But Bonhoeffer's situation confronted him with a horrible choice, whether or not to join a plot against Hitler. Obviously, a plot to kill someone is not congruent with a kingdom of righteousness and peace. But to Bonhoeffer, not joining the conspiracy was worse. He and his co-conspirators relied on deception and violence to lessen the injustice of the world. Of course, the deception and violence of the plot against Hitler were tiny compared to the civilization-shaking violence of the Nazis. Nevertheless, Bonhoeffer and his compatriots chose the power of the sword rather than the power of resurrection.

It seems that when a forced-choice situation arises, a person must either act congruently with her hope or abandon the hope. At some point, one can't continue to hold both the hope and the backup plan. But . . .

Perhaps Bonhoeffer would say he did. Certainly, he still hoped for God's kingdom to come; it's just that in this case he couldn't act congruently with his hope. How far can one act against one's hope and still hold that hope?

Another way to conceptualize the problem is in terms of conflicting virtues. A good person lives in hope *and* pursues justice. (Other virtues, e.g., integrity, might also conflict with hope.) "Hope for the best," says Adrienne Martin, "but prepare for the worst." So, we hope for peace and reconciliation or some other good, but we prepare to shoot the intruder. Thus, many Christians in this country affirm that they follow Jesus, but they keep deadly weapons ready to protect their property. They are willing to use these weapons; else, why prepare them? The implicit judgment here is that justice (preventing theft, for example) requires violence.

And so, in one small step after another, practicing Christians step away from resurrection hope. We continue to hope that we will be raised, but we cease to hope that God's kingdom will come by resurrection power. Like the worldly wise, we think that security, justice, and peace come from coercion, violence, and manipulation.

I have used peacemaking and violence to illustrate the challenge of resurrection hope, but I want to be clear. Resurrection hope generates many such challenges, because resurrection hope has other aspects. Precisely because we hope for a kingdom of righteousness, peace, and joy, an ethic based on Christian hope will be complex.

An example: N. T. Wright presses hard on economics, the realm of international trade and debt. What do we hope for in the coming kingdom? Will there be poverty and extreme disparity of wealth in the resurrection age? Of course not. But if we look forward to a new heaven and earth where the blessed community dwells, why do we not help the millions of fellow Christians who live in poverty now?

Wright does not call for radical redistribution of wealth. But he points out that international systems of debt force governments to prioritize debt repayment over education, medicine, and basic needs of poor people. Should not Christians in wealthy countries such as the United Kingdom urge their governments and international agencies like the World Bank to forgive loans, to lighten the load on the poor?[9]

"Realists," some of them Christians, object to Wright's pleas. That's not the way international markets work, they say. Realists say, debt forgiveness won't work; it will just enrich and reward the (often corrupt) upper classes in developing countries. Some Christians say: the blessed community comes in heaven, not now. Wright responds: all these arguments (and more) were used against John Woolman and William Wilberforce 200 years ago, yet the slave trade *was* stopped by Christians who grounded their opposition to slavery in Christian hope. Wright contends that international debt relief is a twenty-first-century issue parallel to slavery in the nineteenth century. If we hope for a blessed community, we ought to act in accord with that hope.

Consider one last illustration of the challenge of Christian hope, this time not on a state or international scale, but on a personal level: end-of-life

9. Wright, *Surprised by Hope*, 216–20.

care. Modern medicine has confronted millions of Christians with decisions unknown by previous generations. Should we use a certain procedure or drug or machine to prolong life? The diagnosis may be cancer, leukemia, diabetes, or some other. The medical experts can only give probabilities: this course of treatment has this range of expected outcomes, while an alternative course of treatment has another range of outcomes.

Some patients will not be able to consult with doctors or decide their treatment in the time of crisis. We may be unconscious or in some other way incompetent to decide for ourselves. Therefore, we prepare ahead. We have become accustomed to a new feature in modern medicine, the Advance Directive (or Living Will). Millions of people have signed advance directives, which inform physicians of the patients' desires in regard to treatment. Widespread now, advance directives were only first proposed in 1969.

What values or desires drive individuals' decisions when they prepare their living wills? What do they want from modern medicine? In most cases, patients want to live. But they also want to avoid pain. They want to be able; they don't want treatments that greatly interfere with living as they choose. And financial considerations matter too; patients do not want to empty their estates, robbing their legatees, to buy a few months of life. Thus, for many people medical planning becomes an exercise in balancing competing desires. They are willing to live somewhat shorter lives if by doing so they enhance quality of life and/or protect their estates for legatees.

How should Christian hope influence our thinking about medical procedures in general and end-of-life care in particular? We might expect Christians to think much like other people, balancing desire for longer life with desires to avoid pain and disability. Is there nothing more to be said? I think there is. The aspects of Christian hope mentioned above should shape our thinking in at least four ways.

First, and most obviously, we *need not fear death*. Since we hope for eternal life in resurrected bodies, the length of this life matters little. Are these just fine words or "whistling in the dark?" Not if we judge by evidence. The history of Christianity is replete with examples of persons who died without fear precisely because they hoped for resurrection life. John Donne's famous sonnet, "Death Be Not Proud," expresses the confidence of past millions:

> Death, be not proud, though some have called thee
> Mighty and dreadful, for thou are not so;

For those whom thou think'st thou does overthrow
Die not, poor Death, nor canst thou kill me.
. . . .
One short sleep past, we wake eternally
And death shall be no more; Death, thou shalt die.[10]

Second, Christians *should not fear dependence*. On this point, Christian hope runs counter to the ideas of many of our contemporaries, perhaps especially in America. Influenced by slogan words such as "autonomy" or "independence," people in our time express fear of "becoming a burden." When preparing an advance directive, such people may forbid medical interventions if those procedures will leave them unable to care for themselves. Their self-concept is essentially individualistic; for them, a community is nothing more than a collection of individuals. An individual who must depend on others falls short of the ideal.

Against such sociological atomism, Christian hope promises that we will participate in a blessed community. In the life to come we will know others and be known. We will love and be loved. None of us will be independent of others. Since we will be a genuine community in the resurrection, we should not fear dependence now.

For too many in our culture, "independence" is an idol. They worship something that doesn't exist, for all people are dependent on others; some merely hide the truth from themselves. Of all people, philosophers especially ought to be aware of our interdependence. The problems about which we think and the concepts and tools we use to think about them are all inherited from others.[11] When people believe, falsely, in their self-sufficiency, they may hasten their deaths to avoid dependency.

Christians are free to acknowledge the truth. We are, in fact, dependent creatures. If, in the process of dying, our dependence on others becomes more obvious, it is only a revealing of what has always been the case. Just as it is a privilege to render care to the dying, it is a mark of humility and realism to accept such care. Giving and receiving care in this life anticipates the resurrection community.

Third, Christian hope implies that we should *live lightly on the earth*. It is unfortunately true that some Christians have reasoned that because

10. Donne, "Death Be Not Proud," lines 1–4, 13–14.

11. For a philosophical discussion of the depth of human interdependence, see MacIntyre, *Dependent Rational Animals*.

Jesus will come to save us, we therefore need not care for God's creation. But Christian hope includes hope for cosmic redemption, a "new heaven and earth." To be sure, the hope for something new means the old will pass away, but that doesn't mean the old should be polluted or devalued.

The hope of resurrection implies both connection and change between our physical bodies now and our spiritual bodies to come. In a similar way, Paul says that the whole creation groans as it waits for liberation from decay (Rom 8:20–23). We are to be stewards and caretakers of God's creation as it is now in preparation for whatever responsibilities we may have in the creation as it will be.

Fourth, Christian hope gives us resources for *realistic grief*. We look forward to resurrection life and a blessed community, but for as long as we live in the present age, we experience loss. Hope does not deny the reality of loss or paper it over with happy talk. People grieve, and rightly grieve, over many things: broken relationships, the loss of productive labor, incomplete or failed projects, and so on. Children grieve too: moving away from friends, the death of a pet, and other "small" losses—and the adults in the children's lives need to be alert to them.

Death is chief among our griefs. The longer we live, the more occasions we have to grieve death. Parents, teachers, siblings, spouses, children, partners, and friends—no relationship is safe. Death seemingly destroys the best parts of good lives.

Christian hope does not deny grief or say that the losses aren't real. Christian hope helps us *complete* our grief.[12] We sorrow for the things left unsaid, the apologies we didn't make, and the love we didn't express. Grief recovery therapists encourage grieving persons to say or write out such things, to give words to the emotions of grief. Words spoken or written to the deceased function symbolically, helping us move toward "completion." Christian hope tells us that our words are not symbols only; in the resurrection we will be able to say what we wished we had said.

Recapitulation

Any ethic of hope depends on the object-state one hopes for, and it will face dilemmas of forced choice in which persons must choose between acting toward/for the desired object-state and acting on some backup plan. Christian hope aims for a complex object-state, which encompasses

12. James and Friedman, *Grief Recovery Handbook*, 115–50.

resurrection of the body, eternal life, a blessed community, and a new/restored creation. Christians should seek to live into their hope; they should resolutely resist the wisdom of the world that seeks security, peace, and justice by means of manipulation and violence. Christian hope should free us from fear of death and the temptations of "independence." Christian hope should motivate us to care for the creation around us and enable us to be realistic in our grief.

Personal Note

Philosophical work is always affected by practical living. The appendix to this book contains essays I wrote in the months before and after the 2016 death of my wife, Karen Bates-Smith. The "Last Walk" essays do not solve the problem of death and grief; they are the record of one Christian's experience of hope.

The Last Walk

T he "Last Walk" essays first appeared on my blog, storyandmeaning. blogspot.com. With a handful of edits, they appear here as I wrote them at the time.

The Last Walk 1

July 28, 2016

Life overtakes philosophy. For two years I have been reading and thinking about the virtue of hope. I've posted dozens of hope essays on my blog and read two papers at professional philosophy conferences. Eventually, I will write a book on this virtue. But moral philosophy is *practical* (a theme in all my books on the virtues, beginning with *Learning to Love*). It turns out that I am exploring hope in a very personal way.

Background: In 2013, my wife Karen was diagnosed with endometrial cancer, involving three types of cancer cells: endometrial, serous, and clear cell. The first is most common, the second and third more dangerous. She underwent surgery in September, followed by many weeks of chemotherapy and radiation. The treatment regimen lasted until April 2014. Chemotherapy stole her hair, but in Karen's experience radiation therapy was much harder, leaving her with intestinal problems for months afterward. Still, by summer 2014 she was back at work as a psychological disability examiner. And she was sixty-two. She decided to retire.

That fall Karen began a new career as a freelance photographer. She took art photos and portrait photos. She took photography courses, bought lots of good equipment, and redecorated our living room into a studio. She displayed photos in local coffee shops.

Throughout 2015, "gut" problems persisted. In the decade before her surgery, Karen had enjoyed walking for exercise, going for long (forty-five-minute) vigorous walks in various neighborhoods. But "bowel insecurity" put an end to that. Late in 2015, she experimented with indoor walks at the local Fred Meyer.

After the cancer treatments of thirteen to fourteen, Karen had regular follow-up visits with her oncologist. At the beginning of 2016, her blood work showed no signs of the cancer. Karen's doctor said it was as if she had reached mile twenty-one of a twenty-six-mile marathon. She might really be cancer-free.

In February 2016, Karen began experiencing back pain; later, leg pain as well. Her Fred Meyer walks became too painful to continue. There also seemed to be something wrong with her sinuses; the aroma of most foods became nauseating, which meant that she began eating less. These symptoms all worsened gradually. Doctors prescribed pain medications and ordered CT scans.

Here we are now, summer 2016.

An urgent message from Karen's general practitioner: come and see me right away. The next day, we learned cancer had returned. Four days later we met with the oncologist and Karen was immediately started on chemotherapy. There will be no surgery to remove cancer, since it has spread to too many lymph nodes. The next day, a urologist scheduled Karen for a minor procedure to insert a stent at a place where swollen lymph nodes impeded her ureter.

The oncologist gave straightforward answers to our questions. There is a very small probability that chemotherapy alone can kill the cancer. Much more likely, chemotherapy will let us "manage" or "control" the cancer. "Control" in this context means knocking it back, killing many of the rogue cells. But we should expect, he said, that each round of chemo (using different drugs at different stages) would "train" the cancer to evade the drugs' power. Short of a miracle, the cancer will take Karen's life, most likely in two to five years.

So here we are, two middle-aged people, beginning our last "walk" together. We hope that aggressive pain management might permit literal walks again. We look back on my year-long sabbatical in 2007–08 as a highlight of our marriage; we took many walks that year.

With Karen's permission, I have decided not to keep our story secret. I do not intend to make a spectacle of it. I will occasionally post updates on our experience.

The Last Walk 2

August 4, 2016

> A society grows great when old men plant trees whose shade they know they shall never sit in.
>
> Greek Proverb

> He who plants a tree plants a hope.
>
> Lucy Larcom

Building an addition to one's house isn't quite like planting a tree. In deciding to build, Karen and I justified the expense to ourselves by saying we could recoup our costs someday when we sell it. In theory, adding to one's house is just another investment.

But context changes things; it even changes the meaning of things. The real reason for building an addition, no matter what we told ourselves about resale prices, was to give James and Jennie more room. Our son and daughter-in-law have lived with us for more than a year. They've been careful to keep themselves to their small bedroom, and the addition would give them more space. We contracted with Matthew, our builder—and quickly modified the plan to add a concrete pad for a hot tub. A hot tub, we thought, might help with Karen's persistent back pain.

Then we learned Karen's cancer has returned. We enter a new phase in our life together, our last walk. For Karen especially this changes the meaning of the addition and the hot tub. It changes her garden. (Make no mistake, the flowers, shrubs, trees, and garden paths are all her doing. Sometimes I dig holes where she tells me.) In a few months or years someone else will have her house and garden.

In the long view, this has always been true. We all know we will die someday. We know our houses and gardens will pass to others. Our accomplishments will be forgotten. (Quick! What do you know about your great grandmother's great grandmother? Nothing? Your descendants won't remember you either.)

We know we will die. Usually, we don't think about it. Now that we've come to our last walk, Karen and I have to think about it. We've lived in our house twenty-three years. Who will be here twenty-three years hence? What will they be like? How will they change the garden? Will they like the hot tub?

Of course, the Greek proverb is not only about trees. It's about caring for people we won't live to see, people who won't remember us. We "plant trees" by building houses, growing gardens, teaching children, and so on. There are myriad ways to contribute to a good world for those who come after. One might even "plant a tree" by voting!

The Last Walk 3

August 31, 2016

I suppose if one had much experience with cancer, as oncology professionals do, one would discern a pattern in the progress of the disease. Karen's oncologist, Dr. G, tried to give us a sense of what we could expect. This was in July.

First, he said, there is a small chance chemotherapy would completely kill the cancer. Karen might be cured and live for years. Much more likely, however, chemo treatments would achieve "control" of the cancer. In Dr. G's words, this meant each round of therapy would kill much of the cancer but not eliminate it. We could expect the disease to return every time. By a kind of natural selection, it would return stronger, more able to resist drugs. Eventually, even using different anti-cancer drugs in the chemo cocktail, the disease will kill Karen. "Control" thus means that Karen might live a year or as long as five years. Perhaps 70 percent of cases achieve control.

What Dr. G left unsaid (I'm drawing conclusions on my own here) is that 5 percent plus 70 percent leaves a quarter of the cases in which chemo has little or no effect. Without treatment, Dr. G said, the cancer would kill Karen in six months or less.

The "typical" history of the disease is a generalization from many cases. Dr. G summarized for us not only from his own experience but the medical literature. But Karen's case is not the typical case; it is one particular case. She and I will go through the ups and downs of this cancer, and it's not conforming to expectations.

I had to take Karen to hospital. Here's the story as far as we know it.

Chemo knocks Karen's blood chemistry for a loop. Kills cancer? We hope so. It definitely reduces her hemoglobin. Blood with reduced oxygen-carrying capacity produces deep fatigue. So: cancer leads to chemo, which leads to lowered hemoglobin, which leads to fatigue. She had her first transfusion eighteen days ago.

Karen also takes medications for pain. Lots of them; I won't go into details. Let's just say they are powerful. Pain meds act on her nervous system (duh); combined with the extreme fatigue they interfere with her mental functioning. She starts a thought or a sentence and can't finish. She falls asleep in mid-thought. So: cancer leads to pain meds (+ fatigue), which leads to confusion. After thirty years as a clinical psychologist, this frightens Karen. Most of those years were spent administering neuropsychological tests; she is familiar with the various stages and forms of dementia. On Sunday, amid tears, she feared people using that word about her. It's the drugs, I said. "My brain is structurally sound," she answered, lucid for a few seconds.

Then Karen noticed that her left leg was swollen. That was the last bit of evidence. I took her to hospital. Emergency Room staff worried at first about a blood clot. Testing seemed to show that wasn't the problem, but her kidney function was off. They ordered transport to a larger hospital.

On Monday, at St. Vincent's she had her second transfusion. Over the next two days, her fatigue lessened, but only a little. The hemoglobin problem was solved (temporarily anyway), but pain meds and messed-up blood chemistry were still there. It turns out that chemo sometimes causes certain kidney diseases. Who knew? On Tuesday we thought maybe her chemo cocktail would have to be changed. She's due for chemotherapy next Tuesday.

Tests: ultrasound pointed to problems with the right kidney. They wanted to perform a CT scan "with contrast," which means injecting a special dye into the patient; this test is top of the line. But the dye is nasty stuff and dangerous if the patient's kidneys aren't working properly. On Wednesday, an ordinary CT scan, without contrast, revealed a kidney stone.

Many years ago, my father suffered terribly from kidney stones. But this stone is good news! The problem may be correctable without compromising Karen's chemotherapy. Surgery is scheduled for Thursday. Meanwhile, hospital staff has more carefully calibrated her pain meds, and she sleeps more peacefully. I hope she can come home a day or two after surgery.

The Last Walk 4

September 7, 2016

"Be joyful in hope,
patient in affliction, faithful in prayer."

Rom 12:12

Paul's words present a stiff challenge. Are Karen and I joyful, patient, faithful? Hm. On the last point, many friends have assured us they are praying for Karen and me on our last walk. Prayer is a facet of human solidarity, and we are grateful for our friends' prayers. A week ago, I asked friends to pray that Karen could come home.

Who would have guessed that a kidney stone could be good news? On Thursday, Dr. B operated on Karen's right kidney, removing the stone and placing a stent in her ureter. (Dr. B calls himself the plumbing doctor; he's a urologist, not to be confused with a nephrologist, the kidney expert. In Karen's case, they both are part of a team, of which Dr. G, the oncologist, is head. I'm learning lots of new vocabulary.)

Karen's body chemistry and mental functioning began improving immediately after surgery. During a two-hour visit later Thursday, I witnessed her voice strengthening and her mind clearing. Friday afternoon, when I checked phone messages after class, Jennie, our daughter-in-law, said not to go to the hospital. My sister-in-law Janie had taken Karen home already.

In the five days since then we've been learning to balance pain meds. If she takes too little, Karen's pain spikes, especially if she "does" anything—stand up, dress herself, walk a few steps, etc. Call this Scylla. On the other hand, if we overdo the meds the drugs hammer her cognitive abilities. That's Charybdis. Like Odysseus, we try to navigate between the monster and the whirlpool. Of course, Karen faces complications that Odysseus could never have imagined. For example, after kidney surgery patients sometimes experience sudden, uncontrollable bladder function. That stage has passed, thank God; but we had a series of adventures last Friday night!

Karen was scheduled for a chemo treatment Tuesday, but Dr. G postponed it. It's more important to achieve balance on pain meds. There is clinical evidence that good pain control improves the efficacy of chemotherapy, he says. Karen is learning to judge her pain state more precisely; learning to take the "breakthrough" meds *before* pain increases. We're getting better at pain management, so much so that Karen called Tim and Tia (son and daughter-in-law) to confirm her plan to visit them next week. It's her decision to make, so I will drive to Kennewick on two successive Saturdays, delivering her on the first and retrieving her the next. I expect lots of pictures of Jakobi. Meanwhile, we have had visits from home health care and home health physical therapy.

That's a lot of prayers answered in only a week. "faithful in prayer" sounds like good advice.

The Last Walk 5

September 21, 2016

Cancer complicates life. Daily activities take longer. Every visit to the bath presents danger of falling. The caregiver wants to intervene, to protect against injury. But the patient needs to do as much for herself as she can, to maintain strength, balance, mental agility, etc. In addition to such little complications, there are some big ones. We have to adjust on the fly.

For example, on September 10, I drove Karen to visit Tim and Tia, our son and daughter-in-law, who live in Kennewick. Karen had been looking forward to this trip for weeks. The next day, Sunday, Karen felt sick, with flu symptoms. She didn't want to expose Jakobi, our one-year-old grandson, so she asked Tim to drive her home.

We suspect Karen's symptoms came from having a flu shot. It's wise, of course, for her to have a flu shot; influenza can be fatal to people with weakened immune systems. The downside of inoculation is that people often get mild flu symptoms—but for cancer patients, mild symptoms aren't so mild.

Karen called me when she and Tim set out. I drove east and met Tim and Karen in the tiny town of Rufus, and from there I brought her home. The planned week with Tim and Tia amounted to one night. And for Karen the drive home was thoroughly unpleasant.

Another big adjustment: Janie, my sister-in-law, took Karen for her third chemo treatment yesterday. For a number of reasons Dr. G judged her too weak to receive it. Chemotherapy hits the body hard; the hope is that in doing so it hits the cancer harder. Given Karen's lethargy, mental confusion, dehydration, and other factors, Dr. G said he would not administer the drugs. She was given IV hydration, which helped perk her up, and Dr. G recommended that we ask the home health service to move her to palliative care.

Palliative care, I've learned, is a more intense version of home health care. (As I type this, we're waiting for the nurse's visit.) According to Dr. G, patients under palliative care often improve. He's counting on that, hoping that Karen will be stronger and more alert in two weeks so she can get chemo.

Now when I first heard "palliative care or maybe hospice care" (Janie's phrase on the phone when she told me) my mind latched onto the word "hospice," and I assumed the doctor's advice meant Karen and Phil's last walk would soon end. A later conversation with a home health care supervisor reassured me. It is not unreasonable to expect good results from palliative care. If Karen gets stronger, she may have more chemotherapy. If she gets chemotherapy, it may significantly extend her life.

Now we live in an uncertain space. Will Karen be ready for chemo in two weeks? Is the chemo actually working against the cancer? Tim and Tia plan to come to Newberg soon; will Karen be alert enough to enjoy their visit?

Cancer brings long-term uncertainties too, some of which we can prepare for—reviewing and revising legal documents, buying a burial niche, arranging for cremation, etc. There's a lot of detail work to get ready to die! Yet every conversation is peppered with "if" or "someday" or "eventually." So much we don't know; we don't even know that Karen will die before me, and the documents must reflect that possibility.

When you think about it, cancer only reveals something that is true of every life. We all live in uncertain space. The vibrantly healthy college students in my classroom eagerly make plans for the weekend, the holidays, or their careers after graduation. God bless them—I hope their plans bear fruit as they expect. But the truth is that we do not know what tomorrow will bring. Three weeks, three months, or three years: cancer makes our uncertain space plain to Karen and me. What we can be sure of is how we face the uncertainty. I will love Karen to the end, no matter what. Because of the gospel of Christ, we hope for resurrection, no matter what.

The Last Walk 6

October 5, 2016

Dozens of people have told me they are praying for Karen, including my friend Anis in Bangladesh. Karen has international prayer support!

Nevertheless, her condition deteriorated after her chemotherapy was pushed back from September 20 to October 6. It became clear she would not be able to endure the harsh cocktail of poisons modern medicine uses as its main weapon against cancer. And she herself said she didn't want more chemo.

So, we transferred Karen from palliative to hospice care. Thirty-seven years ago, when Karen was a psychology graduate student, she volunteered in an early hospice program. The cutting-edge medicine of 1979 has been standardized. The hospice people know what they're doing.

Hospice care focuses on comfort, not cure. The goal is to reduce the pain and anxiety at the end of life. The intake nurse explained the program and made changes in Karen's pain management plan. Instead of pills she had to swallow, the intake nurse ordered liquid painkillers. (For the most part, the same meds as before, but much easier to take in liquid form.) Later in the day, a deliveryman set up a hospital bed. Tomorrow, Karen's primary hospice nurse will make his first visit, review the care plan, and make sure we know how to administer liquid pain meds. Nursing assistants will come twice a week to help with bathing, shampoos, and whatnot.

No one can tell how long she will live. In July Dr. G said chemotherapy might give us a year or two. In a few cases, even with metastasized cancer, it provides a cure. Obviously, that did not happen this time. We still live with uncertainty, but the range of possibilities is shrinking. Our last walk will be much shorter than I hoped.

So why doesn't God answer all those prayers? Didn't Jesus promise that the Father would grant anything Jesus' disciples asked for? Is it really God's will for Karen to suffer as she does? As a philosopher I find such questions . . . interesting and worthy of discussion. If the questions are supposed to convey arguments, I don't think the arguments will hold water. As a man whose heart is breaking, I find such questions express only a part of what I feel.

I worship a man who let his enemies kill him. Given the solidarity of the human race, I must be included among those enemies. While he suffered our hate, that man cried out to God, "Why have you forsaken me?" The man I worship faced despair greater than I will ever know, and he triumphed by dying and rising again. By death and resurrection, he has conquered me—and he conquers my fears.

Karen and I will part soon. Our last walk will end. For now.

The Last Walk 7

October 12, 2016

In spring 1976, Eugene McCarthy brought his presidential campaign to Oregon! In doing so, he changed my life.

To explain this, I have to provide background. Some historical context: Eugene McCarthy played an important role in American politics when, as a Democratic Senator, he challenged President Johnson in the New Hampshire primary. McCarthy lost the primary, but Johnson's narrow margin of victory helped convince him to not run for reelection.

"Wait a moment!" you might object. "McCarthy challenged Johnson in 1968, but you mentioned 1976." And you would be right. McCarthy's fifteen minutes of fame (according to Andy Warhol, in the future we will all be famous for fifteen minutes) came in 1968. For a few months in that awful year McCarthy was a major political figure in this country.

[Brief side comment: many of us are deeply troubled by presidential politics this year, as we should be. But if you can, recall 1968: Vietnam war going full blast, MLK assassinated, Robert Kennedy assassinated, the Democratic convention and "the whole world is watching," and Richard Nixon picking Spiro Agnew to be Vice President. As bad as 2016 seems, things could be worse.]

In 1976, Eugene McCarthy was not a major political figure. But like other politicians he had caught the presidential bug, and he could not let go of the dream. He soldiered on, taking his 1976 campaign to the little places away from the bright lights. One of those places was Linfield College, where he would make a speech to college students. Students from many Oregon colleges were invited to attend.

George Fox College History professor Ralph Beebe jumped on the opportunity. McCarthy wasn't important in 1976, but only eight years before McCarthy had helped pull down a wartime president. Ralph urged George Fox College students to drive to Linfield to hear McCarthy's speech. Naturally, I went. McCarthy's speech was totally forgettable, proven by the fact I remember nothing he said.

After McCarthy's speech, attending students were divided randomly into discussion groups and sent to various classrooms in Melrose Hall. And that's when magic happened. There was a girl in my group (about twenty-five students) who contributed insightful comments to the discussion—and to my surprise she identified herself as a George Fox student.

George Fox College in the 1970s was much smaller than today. I thought I knew everybody. Yet here was this smart—and very pretty—young woman whom I hadn't met! I came back to campus with a mission to find out about Karen Bates. It turned out that she had transferred to Fox from another college, and she lived off campus, which explained why I didn't know her. I asked her for a date. We rode bicycles to Champoeg Park. (I had to borrow a bike for this purpose.) Afterward, she kissed me on the back porch of her parents' house. Later that year, in summer, I said to her, "If things keep going this way, I'm going to ask you to marry me." She said that would be okay.

Let it not be said that presidential candidates never accomplish good things. In 1976, Eugene McCarthy did good.

Karen Bates-Smith died on October 9, 2016. I miss her terribly.

The Last Walk 8

Eulogy at St. Peter Church

I can't possibly say all I would like to say about Karen, so I will talk about her life as a Catholic.

Karen Suzanne Bates was born February 4, 1952, to Glenn and Betty Bates in The Dalles, Oregon. She grew up attending Conservative Baptist churches in The Dalles, McMinnville, and Newberg. Years later, she told me she and other Newberg High students would debate rather fine points of theology between classes. It seemed important to her at the time to be right, theologically, and she was happy to defend every point of Conservative Baptist doctrine. Karen was very smart; I don't imagine she lost many debates. In 1970, she was NHS valedictorian.

In the early 1970s, Karen experienced an abusive, violent, and short marriage. The trauma of those years pushed her toward studying psychology and sparked spiritual searching. In 1977, Karen married me and changed her name to Karen Bates-Smith. In marrying me, she became a Quaker. It turned out that though she was content with me for a husband, she wasn't fully content as a Friend.

Three months after marrying, we entered Fuller Theological Seminary. The psychology PhD program at Fuller takes six years. Students earn an MA degree in theology, in addition to their work in psychology, during their four years of course work. The last two years are spent in internships and—for most Fuller students—dissertation writing. Karen finished her course work *and* her dissertation in the four years. And she also had a baby, our son Tim.

Already, in our Pasadena years, Karen started visiting Catholic churches. She did this on her own. As a couple we were active in the Friends Church; for our last two years I was pastor of Pasadena Friends. But Karen was already feeling a stirring in her heart, something drawing her toward contemplative worship that she found sitting in Mass.

We moved to Portland in 1982. I pastored Maplewood Friends Church, and Karen supported my work in every way she could. She served on a Yearly Meeting board, she hosted meetings in our house, she played piano for Sunday worship, and—perhaps most important, given the tiny salary the church could afford to pay me—she earned most of the family income.

In the late eighties I left the pastorate to pursue philosophy at the University of Oregon and an increased teaching load at George Fox. Karen shifted the focus of her psychology practice to neuropsychological testing. For many years she worked for Disability Determination Services and later, in private practice, as a consultant for DDS. We adopted our second son, James, in 1989.

Since I was no longer a Friends pastor, Karen felt greater freedom to pursue her spiritual stirrings toward Catholic worship. We moved to Newberg in 1989. She drove to St. John Fisher in Portland for RCIA. At Easter, 1991, she was formally confirmed as a member of the Catholic Church. For a year or two, she attended St. Francis church in Sherwood before finally settling in St. Peter Church here in Newberg.

Karen worried that by becoming a Catholic she would impede my career at George Fox. She knew about anti-Catholic thinking among some Protestants. When I was finishing my degree at UO we contemplated moving to various parts of the country. (I applied for lots of philosophy jobs in 1991, even flew to New York to interview for one of them.) She thought, perhaps, that in another location her faith would not be a hindrance.

Intellectually I embraced Catholics as fellow Christians. But emotionally I weathered a storm when Karen entered the church. It was Jesus, I believe, who told me not to argue against Karen's conversion. Her leading was from Christ; I was not to get in the way.

In 1992, it became clear I needed to stay at Fox. We bought a house in Newberg and settled into a two-church routine. Karen attended Mass at St. Peter's on Saturday, and she and I took the boys to Newberg Friends on Sunday. Karen often played cello for Saturday Mass. She wrote music for Mass. Twice a year (Good Friday and Christmas) I attended Mass with Karen. And later, when the boys were grown, whenever we went on vacation, we found it simple to attend Mass—it seems there is always a Catholic church nearby.

Rather than causing a problem, the fact that Karen was a Catholic proved to be a boon to my work as a professor. When some student would express some anti-Catholic prejudice, I could gently raise a concrete example of a Protestant led by God to become a Catholic. I myself could not join the church, but I could love and honor a woman who did. Our marriage became a living illustration of theological inclusivity.

Interestingly, not many of my students have become Quakers. Maybe I should be a better evangelist. But some of my best students, such as Abigail Rine (now Favale) and Angela Wood (now Pearson) have become Catholics. Abby is a professor at GFU. Angela has not finished her doctorate, but she is the happy mother of five children, teaching her toddlers how to say "episteMOLogy."

Karen Bates-Smith obeyed the leading of the Spirit into the Catholic church. From that obedience has come much good for our family, for St. Peter parish, and for my students at Fox. She died October 9, 2016.

The Last Walk 9

Eulogy at Newberg Friends Church

I can't possibly say everything I would like to say about Karen, so I will talk about her life as an artist. We have purchased a burial niche at Newberg Friends Cemetery. The inscription on the niche will say of Karen: "Maker of Beauty."

Karen Bates was born February 4, 1952, to Glenn and Betty Bates in The Dalles, Oregon. She grew up in The Dalles, McMinnville, and Newberg, graduating from Newberg High School in 1970.

Karen demonstrated varied talents at Newberg High School. She competed in gymnastics and scored points for her team on the balance beam. She sang in a high school choral group called "Shades of Blue" that performed in local concerts. She also sang in choirs for high school commencements and a local production of *The Messiah*. She practiced calligraphy and drawing with charcoal.

While still in high school, Karen moved deeper into music. She created an arrangement of "Sunrise, Sunset" for the high school choir and conducted the choir's rendition of the popular song in 1969.

In 1977, Karen married Philip Smith, changing her name to Karen Bates-Smith. In 1981, she gave birth to a son, Tim. In 1989, we adopted a son, James.

After college, Karen attended Fuller Theological Seminary, completing a PhD in psychology in 1983. She made a career as an Oregon licensed psychologist for more than thirty years. But her musical muse would not leave her alone. In the early eighties she bought a cello and started lessons. Pretty soon, she bought a much more expensive cello, and her husband knew the music thing was serious.

In the 1980s, when I was pastor of Maplewood Friends Church, Karen aided worship greatly by playing piano, collaborating with Meredith Fieldhouse, who led singing.

We moved to Newberg in 1989. It wasn't long before Karen joined the Chehelem Symphony, directed by Dennis Hagen. For years she played cello alongside Theo Powers. Besides two or three concerts a year with the Chehelem Symphony, Karen gave solo performances in concerts at the Portland Community Music Center. For a couple years, Theo joined her, giving the Smith and Powers sons a chance to squirm in their seats while their mothers performed.

Karen Bates-Smith, Karen Scott, and Pat Surguy formed a trio (cello, piano, violin) called *Clavis Trio*. They gave recitals at Friendsview Manor and Newberg Friends Church.

By the late nineties, performance wasn't enough. Karen returned to school, pursuing an undergraduate music degree at Marylhurst University, with an emphasis in composition. At first, she focused on choral music, including "Sing to Yahweh," which was performed in worship by the Newberg Friends Choir in June 1998. She also wrote pieces for piano and cello, such as "Sonata #1" which was performed by Theo Powers and Jane Smith in 1998. In her senior recital, in 2002, various musicians performed "Love's Whimsey" (soprano and piano), "Rondo for Alto Flute" (a memorial to victims of 9/11), Rhyme Quintet in E-Flat" (by the Con Grazia Wind Quintet), "String Trio #1 in C Major" (violin, viola, and cello). Karen also wrote music for at events at Warner Pacific College, such as "Brass Ring" for a concert called the Brass Bash.

After finishing at Marylhurst in 2003—her second undergraduate degree—Karen gradually played cello less and concentrated more on composing. Eventually she left the Chehelem Symphony. But she continued to practice cello to keep up her skills. With her friend, Darlene Babin, she practiced a variety of cello and piano pieces, many of them her own compositions. She contributed new work for recitals at Marylhurst, including "Brown and Furry" and "The Telephone Is Under the Stairs" (soprano and piano).

By this point you get the idea: Karen wrote for voices and for a great variety of instrumental combinations: string trios, woodwind quintets, brass groups, orchestras, and so on.

That is not the end of the story. In a sense, it's only half. In 2014, after her first go-round with cancer, Karen retired as a psychologist. Then she went out and bought a camera. She bought another camera. And lenses. And lighting equipment. Her husband knew this photography thing was serious.

Karen opened a business, Take Wing Photography. With our daughter-in-law Jennie's help, she transformed our living room into a portrait studio. She also took her camera to Coffee Cottage and to people's houses. She came back with some penetratingly realistic photos of people. I defy anyone to find a better picture of Ed Higgins than the one Karen captured.

In my opinion, though, Karen's art photography surpassed her portraits. In some cases, she manipulated the camera to achieve pure abstraction. In other pictures, she used extreme close-up shots to bring the viewer intimately into nature. She made pictures that reveal beauties we too often pass by without noticing.

Sadly, Karen's photography career lasted less than two years. Cancer came back. Debilitating pain forced her to stop. October 9, 2016, she died.

I don't know if we will make photos after the resurrection. Scripture strongly hints we will make music. In Tolkien's delightful story, "Leaf by Niggle," the artwork we make here prepares us for greater artmaking in the next life. It will be pure delight to see what Karen's work here might lead to there.

The Last Walk 10

Kingdom Hope

October 26, 2016

Betty Bates, my mother-in-law, died last spring. At the time we did not guess that her daughter, my wife Karen, would die of cancer a few months later. I have had two occasions to think about hope in personal terms, not only as a philosopher.

Death stamps a final "incomplete" on our earthly projects. Karen left music compositions half-edited, letters to her grandson and granddaughter half-written, and photo projects still in the planning stage. The addition to our house, mostly Karen's idea, is still not quite finished. (I need to remind the builder to send an electrician.) Mundane hopes focus on such earthly things. As Karen's cancer advanced, she confided to a friend that she hoped to live until the birth of our second grandson, due in January. Death frustrated that hope.

Paul teaches in 1 Corinthians 15 that the resurrection of Jesus is absolutely fundamental to Christian faith. If Jesus was not raised, he writes, the gospel is false, and we are still in our sins. Further, he says, the resurrection of Jesus grounds the hope that we will be raised. On the basis of this doctrine, it is entirely proper for Christians to hope for a *personal* afterlife. Betty and Karen both died in hope that they would see people they had known and loved in heaven. They hoped also they would *be* known.

Christian hope is personal, but not individualistic. The headline message of Jesus' preaching, according to the Gospels: "Repent! The Kingdom of God is near."

To repent means to change one's whole life, a reorientation of one's values and aims. One aspect of repentance (not the whole) is to change one's thinking. To a degree, the call to repentance is a call to change one's mind. Repentance means we need to learn to think in kingdom terms. And one aspect of that task is to consider how the *kingdom* affects our *hope*.

The "kingdom of God" obviously involves a king and people who are subjects of the king. It is a *social* concept. To live in a kingdom has implications for relationships between the king's subjects. We must treat each other as the king commands.

[An aside. In political imagery, we sometimes contrast the *subjects* of a king or emperor with the *citizens* of a democracy or republic. I prefer the latter to the former; probably you do too. We think citizenship in a republic recognizes human dignity in a way no king or emperor could do. Consider, though, how different the kingdom of God is. According to Paul, it is "righteousness, peace, and joy in the Holy Spirit" (Rom 14). In the kingdom of God, we are all "children" and "heirs" or "brothers/sisters" of the king. The "children" of the kingdom of God enjoy a dignity greater than citizens of earthly republics.]

Justice marks the kingdom of God, right relationships between people. Jesus will come back to rule, to put things right. In biblical words: oppression of the alien or the weak or the orphan will end. In modern terms: fraud, price gouging, loan sharking, mislabeling of products, deceptive contracts, shoddy workmanship, red-lining, racial profiling, cheating of all kinds—all this will end. Justice will reign.

The earth will be *restored*. Biblical visions of the afterlife include a "new heaven and a new earth." "The lion will lie down with the lamb." "They will neither harm nor destroy on all my holy mountain." Again, in our modern terms: pollution of air, land, and water will end. People will live cooperatively with other creatures. We will use the earth without misusing it. We will be gardeners, not exploiters.

It's all just a metaphor, right? Maybe, but maybe not.

As I meditate on the scope of the kingdom metaphor, a truth bears down on me: It's not about me; it's about Jesus. The kingdom of God belongs, in the primary sense, to God. The kingdom of God is something God is doing. I am drawn into it as one of billions of others. I am a part, however small, of the true story.

The true story, the real story, is not about me; it's about Jesus. The story of the kingdom of God is a story with beginning, middle, and end, a story with a plot. The main character is Jesus.

The end of the story is something we hope for. By faith we enter the kingdom now as a present gift of God. But Jesus has not yet returned. Opportunities abound for mockers to ridicule our hope. There is plenty of room and time to experience doubt.

Here is a feature of Christian hope that I had not sufficiently considered: we hope that Jesus will win. We hope the kingdom he proclaimed will in fact come.

Amen. Come, Lord Jesus.

The Last Walk 11
Walking Alone
December 28, 2016

It's been eighty days since Karen died, a bit more than two months since her funeral and memorial services. I am feeling the pain of my loss more acutely than before, not because of Christmas but because of time away from work. I don't have the convenient distractions of class preps and grading of student papers. Other distractions—holiday concerts, parties, church services, and family dinners—are over. Since Christmas I've had some days "off"; something Karen and I used to welcome when we were together, days for walks, for watching a movie, for creative projects. Now, when I walk, I cannot escape the feeling of loss. We used to walk these streets together.

Jerry Sittser, a professor at Whitworth, suffered the simultaneous loss of his mother, wife, and daughter in an auto accident. Four years later he wrote *A Grace Disguised*, and a dozen years after that, *A Grace Revealed*, reflections on God's work in his life after loss. (Thank you to Kris Kays, who lent the books to me.) Sittser says that God can use tragic loss as a means of grace. God wills to redeem us, and he will use even the pain we suffer to work redemption.

Just to be clear: Sittser does not say, and I do not believe, that God changes evil into good. A drunk driver killing three members of Sittser's family was evil. Karen's suffering and death from cancer was a bad thing. The pain I am enduring is not good. "The last enemy to be destroyed is death," wrote Paul, and that means that death is a real enemy—God's enemy as well as ours.

God does not change evil into good, but he uses evil—even the crucifixion of Jesus—to accomplish good. God is changing me, remaking me, through pain. This doesn't mean pain is a good thing or that God is a vindictive wizard toying with me. "God was in Christ, reconciling the world to himself," and he did this by the cross, by suffering with and for us.

I told my sister-in-law, Evie, that there is a temptation to paper over pain and loss. There must be lots of ways to do it. Rush into a new relationship. Spend lots of money. Binge on alcohol, food, exercise, or videos. Bury yourself in work. And so on. The effect is to dull the pain, to not feel. To a degree, distraction works; grading student papers helped me get through the weeks after the memorial. But now the papers and parties are over, leaving me alone.

It's okay to feel loss. At the least, it's *real*. I'm not writing a novel or doing abstract philosophy. (Worthy activities, both of them! But as existentialists point out, sometimes remote from reality.) I cannot rewrite this plot; I cannot cancel my loss. I have to feel it, to let it change me.

How will the new me be different? Over thirty-nine years Karen shaped me in ways I cannot know. I would not want to shed those things. The new me will be changed through addition. Immediately, it seems, I have become more aware of death and the limitations of our existence. Suppose I live as long as my friend Arthur Roberts, who died recently at ninety-three. That would mean two-thirds of my life is already over. Perhaps I will live only as long as my father, in which case four-fifths of my life is over. "Teach us to number our days," say the psalms. The hope of resurrection puts the count of days in new perspective!

As I walk, I feel a new depth of pain. Surely what I feel is not unique! People all around me suffer similar losses. In imagination, at least, the slow loss of a spouse to Alzheimer's would be worse—and I have friends who are on that road. What about divorce? I've only watched from the outside, but it seems that loss (accompanied by resentments, fears, and guilt) could be worse than mine. What about refugees, who lose their countries? Jerry Sittser says such comparisons are pointless; there is no measure of psychic pain with which to compare tragedies. Instead, I should allow God to remake me, to use my pain to spur compassion.

My neighbor, who lost her husband years ago, says, "You don't get over it; you get through it." Jerry Sittser says tragic loss is not like a disease from which you recover; it's like an amputation that leaves you changed. I want to be open to grace, to be changed for the better. The amputation will always be part of me, and I walk on.

The Last Walk 12

A Year Ago Today . . .

September 4, 2017

I expect this will be my last entry under "Last Walk." It's been almost one year since Karen died. For a few weeks now, and especially in the last few days, memory has taken me back to the events of last year.

There is a sense in which years are arbitrary units. Orbits. Why should it matter, in a person's life, whether the earth has completed one of its journeys around the sun? Mercury's orbit is much shorter, Jupiter's much longer. Unless we are astronomers, we pay no attention. We don't *live* on Mercury or Jupiter. Earth's orbit we call a year, and we measure our lives in years.

(Speculation: someday, perhaps in my lifetime, colonists will live on Mars. They will almost certainly live "sols," Martian days roughly thirty minutes longer than Earth's days. Mars takes almost twice as long as Earth to orbit the sun. Will the colonists celebrate Martian birthdays?)

Whether or not a year is an arbitrary length of time, it is built into cultural memes. And since we are social creatures, the cultural meme structures our experience. Without even trying, we inculcate time concepts into our children, as our parents gifted them to us. We *live* in years.

One year ago today . . .

July—Dr. B told Karen cancer had spread to her lymph nodes.

August—Karen underwent chemotherapy and, subsequently, a blood transfusion because the chemo hit so hard.

Early September—Karen's visit to Kennewick was cut short because she felt a cold coming on and didn't want to infect grandson Jakobi.

October 5, a Wednesday—Rich Brown, our lawyer, and a notary public came with documents for Karen to sign. She signed some, but then said she was too tired. We'd do it later, we said. A friend from St. Peter's brought communion.

October 6, Thursday—the hospice people brought a hospital bed. Karen was unconscious all day. We gave her pain meds in liquid form; deposited between cheek and gum, she swallowed them automatically.

October 7, Friday—Ron Mock sat with me most of the morning at Karen's bedside. For a moment she opened her eyes. I told her I loved her. She mouthed words, which Ron and I both thought were, "I love you."

October 8, Saturday—Karen slept all day, breathing slowly.

October 9, Sunday, 9:45 am—Karen stopped breathing. I called hospice, and a nurse came within half an hour. Shortly thereafter, hospice people came to remove Karen's body.

October 20—We attended funeral mass at St. Peter Church.

October 22—Karen's memorial service at Newberg Friends Church.

I have a friend whose husband died more than two years ago. She says the anticipation of the anniversary of death can be harder than the day itself. Maybe so.

I keep Karen's ashes in two beautiful urns, a gift from Mark Terry. The urns stand on top of Karen's rosewood piano. Legally, that piano is mine, but I cannot think of it except as Karen's piano. I bought a niche at the Friends Cemetery; someday, I presume, either I or our sons will move the ashes to the niche.

In my life, the earth will probably orbit the sun twenty or thirty more times. Maybe more, maybe fewer. And that's it, the end; our last walk is finally over. That's what some people say. But I hope . . . well, if you have read these essays, you know about that.

The Last Walk: Epilogue

Resurrection Life

March 5, 2020

Last night I dreamed about Karen. It's been more than three years since she died. I've been married—happily—to Sarah Link for more than a year. The dream didn't grow out of dissatisfaction with my situation.

Admittedly, I don't remember many of my dreams, so it's possible I dream about Karen often. But I don't think so. When I woke up, I realized this dream illustrates an interesting philosophical/theological question.

In the dream some small animal—a dog? cat? squirrel?—somehow found a bit of Karen's body and used that bit to reconstitute Karen. (Bizarre? Sure. It was a dream.) She was alive again, Karen just as she was fourteen months before her death! (Another weird feature of dreams; somehow, I knew it was fourteen months, not a year.)

Karen was reading something; my "Last Walk" essays perhaps. So, Karen in the dream knew the cancer would return, knew when the doctor would tell her she was dying, and knew when she would die. At the same stage in real life Karen knew none of that. Back in 2015, fourteen months before she died, Karen's doctors were pretty confident.

There she was—a resuscitated Karen, with more than a year to live. But dream-Karen was unhappy. I asked her: Didn't she want to live? Her answer: No, not like this.

And there's the question. What do we want—what do Christians hope for—in the afterlife?

In my dream, the magic happened by means of the little animal. Dog, cat, or squirrel—doesn't matter. If you like, you can exchange the animal for a mad scientist, an extraterrestrial invader, or an angel. In the TV series *Stargate*, the aliens had a sarcophagus machine that could re-store dead bodies. I'm not worried about the means; I'm interested in the results. What do we *want* in an afterlife, if there is one?

Christian theologians and Bible scholars insist that real Christian hope centers on resurrection. The same power that raised Jesus from the grave can give life to our bodies too. Of course, we will be *changed*; we will have "spiritual" bodies. (See 1 Cor 15.)

And that's the problem with dream-Karen. She was resuscitated, not resurrected. Somehow the animal or magic had rebuilt her body as she was fourteen months before her death, cancer and all. She was not changed. She had to live her dying months all over again—only worse this time, since in the dream she knew what was going to happen.

When I hope for resurrection, I hope for new life. Not just "new life" in the abstract; *I* want to live. I want to live with others, people I have known and especially Christ himself—I want *community*. So, somehow, I hope that the real me, along with real others, will live again. But I do not hope for resuscitation, a kind of bare-bones new life. I want something better.

The New Testament promises a new heaven and a new earth. The community is symbolized as a city, the New Jerusalem. Since God is an infinite being, I imagine we will be learning forever; our fellowship will be always deepening.

Dream-Karen was right to reject resuscitation, even if she were to be resuscitated over and over. Don't misunderstand my point. I am not saying our life now is valueless. The life God has given us here and now in this world is a wonderful thing. But Christian hope is not just for more years. We would not be satisfied if alien machines or magic animals gave us an unlimited number of do-overs. We want true resurrection, in which the power of God translates us into a new kind of life.

Bibliography

Adams, Robert M. *Finite and Infinite Goods*. Oxford: Oxford University Press, 1999.

Andre, MJ. "Summa Theologica—Question 40 of the Irascible Passions, and First, of Hope and Despair (In Eight Articles)." https://mjandre.com/2019/09/01/summa-theologica-question-40-of-the-irascible-passions-and-first-of-hope-and-despair-in-eight-articles/.

Anscombe, G. E. M. "Modern Moral Philosophy." *Philosophy* 33.124 (1958) 1–19.

Bernier, Mark. *The Task of Hope in Kierkegaard*. Oxford: Oxford University Press, 2015.

Bishop, Michael. *The Good Life: Unifying the Philosophy and Psychology of Well-Being*. Oxford: Oxford University Press, 2015.

Brei, Andrew T., ed. *Ecology, Ethics, and Hope*. New York: Rowman & Littlefield, 2016.

British Medical Association. *The British Medical Association Illustrated Medical Dictionary*. London: Dorling Kindersley, 2002.

Critchley, Simon. "Abandon (Nearly) All Hope." *New York Times*, April 19, 2014. http://opinionator.blogs.nytimes.com/2014/04/19/abandon-nearly-all-hope/.

Darabont, Frank, dir. *The Shawshank Redemption*. Culver City, CA: Columbia Pictures, 1994.

Donne, John. "Death Be Not Proud." https://www.poetryfoundation.org/poems/44107/holy-sonnets-death-be-not-proud.

Drefeinski, Shane. "A Very Short Primer on St. Thomas Aquinas' Account of the Various Virtues." *Sophia Project Philosophy Archives*, 2015. http://www.sophia-project.org/uploads/1/3/9/5/13955288/drefcinski_virtues.pdf.

Elliot, David. *Hope and Christian Ethics*. Cambridge: Cambridge University Press, 2017.

Frankl, Victor. *Man's Search for Meaning*. London: Rider, 2008.

Hallie, Philip. *Lest Innocent Blood Be Shed*. New York: Harper Colophon, 1979.

Hayes, Chris. "The Idea That the Universe Bends towards Justice Is Inspiring. It's Also Wrong." *Think*, March 24, 2018. https://www.nbcnews.com/think/opinion/idea-moral-universe-inherently-bends-towards-justice-inspiring-it-s-ncna859661#:~:text=Chris%20Hayes%3A%20The%20idea%20that,It's%20also%20wrong.

James, John W., and Russell Friedman. *The Grief Recovery Handbook*. 20th Anniversary Expanded Edition. New York: HarperCollins, 2009.

Kierkegaard, Søren. *Fear and Trembling*. Translated by Sylvia Walsh. New York: Cambridge University Press, 2006.

Lear, Jonathan. *Radical Hope: Ethics in the Face of Cultural Devastation*. Cambridge: Harvard University Press, 2006.

Lopez, Shane J., et al. "Diagnosing for Strengths: On Measuring Hope Building Blocks." In *Handbook of Hope: Theory, Measures, and Applications*, edited by C. R. Snyder, 57–85. San Diego: Academic, 2000.

———. "Hope Therapy: Helping Clients Build a House of Hope." In *Handbook of Hope: Theory, Measures, and Applications*, edited by C. R. Snyder, 123–50. San Diego: Academic, 2000.

MacIntyre, Alasdair. *Dependent Rational Animals*. Chicago: Carus, 1999.

Martin, Adrienne. *How We Hope: A Moral Psychology*. Princeton: Princeton University Press, 2014.

Nolt, John. "Hope, Self-Transcendence, and Environmental Ethics." In *Ecology, Ethics, and Hope*, edited by Andrew T. Brei, 43–63. New York: Rowman & Littlefield, 2016.

Nussbaum, Martha. *The Fragility of Goodness: Luck and Ethics in Greek Tragedy and Philosophy*. Rev. ed. Cambridge: Cambridge University Press, 2001.

Pinches, Charles. "On Hope." In *Virtues and Their Vices*, edited by Kevin Timpe and Craig A. Boyd, 349–68. Oxford: Oxford University Press, 2014.

Popper, Karl. *The Open Society and Its Enemies*. Princeton: Princeton University Press, 1994.

Russell, Bertrand. *A Free Man's Worship*. Portland, ME: Mosher, 1923.

Sachs, Jeffrey D. *The End of Poverty: Economic Possibilities for Our Time*. New York: Penguin, 2005.

Scioli, Anthony, and Henry B. Biller. *Hope in the Age of Anxiety*. Oxford: Oxford University Press, 2009.

Smith, Philip D. *Why Faith Is a Virtue*. Eugene, OR: Wipf & Stock, 2014.

Snyder, C. R., ed. *Handbook of Hope: Theory, Measures, and Applications*. San Diego: Academic, 2000.

Snyder, C. R., and Julia D. Taylor. "Hope as a Common Factor across Psychotherapy Approaches: A Lesson from the Dodo's Verdict." In *Handbook of Hope: Theory, Measures, and Applications*, edited by C. R. Snyder, 89–122. San Diego: Academic, 2000.

Wright, N. T. *Surprised by Hope: Rethinking Heaven, the Resurrection, and the Mission of the Church*. New York: HarperCollins, 2008.